The 202

MW01591846

Encyclopedia of

Serial Killers:

Serial Killers from

A to Z

by

Jack Vale

ISBN: 9798874147549

The Murderer's Index

A: *Albert DeSalvo*

B: *David Berkowitz*

C: *Richard Cottingham*

D: *Jeffrey Dahmer*

E: *Elias Abuelazam*

F: *George Fitzsimmons*

G: *Donald Henry Gaskins*

H: *Fritz Haarmann*

I: *Miyuki Ishikawa*

J: *Keith Hunter Jesperson*

K: *Edmund Kemper*

L: *Henry Lee Lucas*

M: *Herbert Mullin*

N: *Earle Nelson*

O: *The Ominous Outsiders*

P: *Christopher Peterson*

Q: *Questions and Quandaries in Serial Killer Profiling*

R: *Gary Ridgway*

S: *Tommy Lynn Sells*

T: *Ottis Toole*

U: *Unidentified Serial Killers*

V: *Dorángel Vargas*

W: *Women Who Kill - The Female Serial Killer*

X: *The X-Factor in Serial Killing*

Y: *Yang Xinhai*

Z: *Zhang Yongming*

A: *Albert DeSalvo*

Terror in Boston: DeSalvo's Reign

The streets of Boston in the early 1960s became a canvas for a macabre tapestry woven with fear and violence. The predator, lurking in the shadows, was a figure who would soon be etched into the annals of criminal history as the Boston Strangler. His hunting ground was the homes of unsuspecting women, where he left a trail of terror and blood.

The Strangler's method was chilling in its intimacy and brutality. He slipped into the homes of women like a phantom, using charm or deceit to gain entry. Once inside, the facade of normalcy crumbled, revealing a monster driven by a need to dominate and destroy. His victims, aged from 19 to 85, were found in their most private sanctuaries, their bodies a testament to his rage. Strangled with their own clothing, their final moments were an agonizing dance with death, often accompanied by sexual assault.

DeSalvo's reign of terror was marked by a perverse artistry. He didn't just kill; he staged a horrifying show for the world to see. The oldest victim was found dead of a heart attack, a silent scream etched on her face, while others bore the marks of strangulation, stabbing, and beating. The absence of forced entry suggested a sinister truth – these women had looked into the eyes of their killer and seen someone they could trust, not the harbinger of their demise.

As the body count rose, so did the fear. A city held hostage by an unseen menace, mothers, daughters, and sisters lived in a constant state of vigilance. The Strangler's ability to blend into the fabric of everyday life made him even more terrifying. He was the neighbor, the stranger on the street, the unnoticed passerby – a lethal chameleon in a city of unsuspecting prey.

The capture of DeSalvo did little to dispel the horror that had gripped Boston. The stories of his early life painted a picture of a man molded by violence and abuse, a soul corrupted early on. Yet, even as he sat behind bars, the debate raged on – was he the true face behind the Boston Strangler? Or was he a troubled man, confessing to crimes he didn't commit? The enigma of DeSalvo added a final, unsettling layer to the nightmare he had wrought, leaving a lingering question in the shadows of Boston's streets: was the real monster still out there?

Victims' Voices

In the heart of Boston, a city once bustling with life, a sinister shadow loomed, bringing with it a chilling hush. The Boston Strangler's spree was not merely a series of killings; it was a brutal orchestration of terror, marked by a distinct and horrifying signature. Each scene was a grotesque tableau, the victims' lifeless bodies speaking volumes of their final, harrowing moments.

Anna Slesers, 55, was the first to fall prey to this terror. Found in her apartment, her life extinguished by the very fabric of her own clothing, her demise marked the beginning of a series of heinous acts. Each woman, in the sanctity of her home, faced a nightmarish end. The killer's method was perverse in its intimacy – strangulation, an act that requires close proximity, a personal invasion of space, and a horrifying finality in the eyes of the victim.

The residences of these women became stages for a macabre performance, each crime scene meticulously devoid of forced entry, implying a disturbing level of trust or deceit employed by the killer. The Strangler didn't just violate lives; he shattered the sanctity of homes, turning havens into tombs. His methods varied from strangulation to stabbing, but each act was a twisted demonstration of control and power.

In this reign of terror, the city's heartbeat stuttered with fear. Each report of a new victim sent ripples of dread through Boston's streets. Women double-checked locks, eyeing every visitor with suspicion, haunted by the thought of the Strangler's hands reaching for them next. The media's frenzy only intensified the fear, painting a picture of a monster lurking in the most mundane corners of everyday life.

The finality of the Strangler's grip left a city in mourning, families shattered, and a legacy of terror that would linger for decades. These were not mere statistics; they were mothers, daughters, sisters – each with a story brutally cut short. As the sun set on Boston in those years, the darkness brought a palpable sense of dread, a reminder of the horror that had walked its streets.

Capturing a Phantom

The elusive Boston Strangler's reign of terror culminated not in a grand standoff but in a series of seemingly disconnected events that eventually led to his capture. It was a chilling journey from shadow to substance, unraveling a mystery that had held a city in its grip. The manhunt was intense and fraught with false leads and dead ends, a testament to the cunning of the perpetrator.

He, a chameleon in the urban landscape, had managed to avoid detection with a disturbing ease. The police, grappling with the complexities of the case, were often left grasping at straws. It was a struggle against an enemy who was seemingly always one step ahead, blending seamlessly into the city's fabric.

The breakthrough came unexpectedly, not through the Strangler cases, but through a series of sexual assaults by an individual known as the "Green Man." The police's attention was drawn to this man, whose methods bore a striking resemblance to the Strangler's. It was a convergence of paths that led them to a suspect – Albert DeSalvo.

His arrest was not a moment of triumph but one of grim realization. The pieces of the puzzle, once disjointed and perplexing, began to form a coherent, albeit horrifying, picture. The interrogation room became the stage where the phantom finally took form, as DeSalvo's confessions began to peel back the layers of horror that had enveloped Boston.

The capture brought a mixture of relief and revulsion. Relief, that the predator was no longer at large; revulsion, at the magnitude of his crimes. Boston could finally exhale, but the breath was tainted with the grief and horror of the Strangler's ghastly work.

DeSalvo's Mind: Unraveling the Mystery

In the confines of a cold, sterile interrogation room, the enigma of Albert DeSalvo began to unravel. His confessions, a tapestry of horrors, painted a portrait of a man whose psyche was as labyrinthine as the crimes he described. Each word he uttered was a descent into a mind marred by violence and darkness.

His eyes, often described as the windows to the soul, reflected a chilling emptiness. As he recounted his deeds, the air grew heavy with the weight of his words. The investigators listened, horrified, as he detailed each crime with a disturbing calmness and precision. The descriptions were not just clinical; they were intimate, as if he relished reliving each moment.

The complexity of his character was baffling. Here was a man who committed unspeakable acts, yet spoke of them with an almost detached curiosity. It was as if he was exploring his own mind, trying to understand the impulses that drove him. His confessions were punctuated by moments of startling insight, suggesting a self-awareness that was as surprising as it was unsettling.

Yet, within this seeming self-awareness lurked a paradox. DeSalvo's assertions of guilt were met with skepticism by some who saw them as an elaborate fabrication, a final act of manipulation. The inconsistencies in his stories, coupled with the lack of physical evidence, cast a shadow of doubt over his claims.

The quest to understand DeSalvo's mind became a journey into the abyss. The more the investigators learned, the more elusive the truth seemed. He remained a puzzle, a complex blend of brutality and contradiction. In the end, the question lingered: was he a remorseless predator or a troubled soul ensnared by his own demons? The answer, like the man himself, remained shrouded in mystery.

The Making of The Boston Strangler

In the darkness of Boston's underbelly, a sinister figure emerged, his actions painting a chilling portrait of terror. Albert DeSalvo, known infamously as the Boston Strangler, wove a tapestry of horror through the streets, leaving a trail of unspeakable atrocities. The city, once a bustling hub of life and activity, became his hunting ground, its residents unwitting players in his macabre game.

His victims, women from various walks of life, met their end in a manner most gruesome. Their final moments, filled with terror and pain, were a stark contrast to the normalcy of their everyday lives. The Strangler's method was personal and invasive – a cold, calculated strangulation that left its mark both physically and psychologically on the city's consciousness.

The fear he instilled was palpable, a tangible cloud hanging over the city. Women locked their doors and peered through curtains with suspicion, the shadow of the Strangler looming large in their minds. His ability to strike at will, leaving little evidence behind, only added to the growing dread. The city was in the grip of a nightmare, the perpetrator of which seemed like a ghost, slipping away unseen after each horrific act.

In each crime scene, the Strangler left his signature – a gruesome tableau that spoke volumes of his cruelty. The rooms bore silent witness to the struggles that had taken place, the victims' lifeless bodies a testament to his brutality. Each scene was a disturbing insight into the mind of a killer whose appetite for violence knew no bounds.

The hunt for the Strangler was a journey through a labyrinth of fear and mystery. Detectives scoured the city, following leads that often led nowhere, the elusive killer always one step ahead. The city held its breath, waiting for the next strike, the next clue, the next chapter in a saga of terror that had no end in sight.

B: *David **Berkowitz***

The Son of Sam Attacks: A City in Fear

The summer night air was thick with tension, its stillness shattered by sudden, deafening gunshots. In the Pelham Bay neighborhood of the Bronx, Donna Lauria and her friend Jody Valenti sat in a car, their conversation abruptly ended. A figure emerged from the shadows, a .44 caliber Bulldog revolver in hand, and without hesitation, unleashed a torrent of violence. Lauria, an 18-year-old emergency medical technician, was struck by a fatal bullet, her life extinguished in an instant. Valenti, wounded, could only watch in horror as the assailant vanished into the night, leaving behind a scene of chaos and the beginning of a reign of terror in New York City.

The shootings continued, each marked by the same ruthless precision. Carl Denaro and Rosemary Keenan, absorbed in each other's company in Flushing, Queens, found their world explode in shards of glass and blood. Denaro, a 20-year-old security guard, suffered a bullet wound to his head, narrowly escaping death. The city's heart pounded with fear, its streets morphing into a hunting ground for the relentless predator now known as the Son of Sam.

In Floral Park, high school students Donna DeMasi and Joanne Lomino's laughter was cut short by the approach of a man in military fatigues, his voice eerily high-pitched as he began to ask for directions. Before they could react, the revolver appeared, its shots echoing through the night. Lomino was left paralyzed, her dreams shattered along with her spine. The city's soul was gripped by panic, its citizens held hostage by the whims of a merciless gunman.

The terror peaked in the sultry heat of July 1977. Stacy Moskowitz and Robert Violante, enveloped in the innocence of a first date in Bath Beach, Brooklyn, were the next victims. The night's romantic whispers were brutally interrupted as four rounds tore through the car, a brutal punctuation to their budding romance. Moskowitz, a vibrant 20-year-old, succumbed to her injuries, while Violante was left blinded, their lives forever altered by the cruelty of a man whose heart seemed devoid of empathy.

The city's psyche was scarred, its streets no longer symbols of freedom but corridors of fear. Women sheared their long, dark hair, seeking to evade the killer's gaze. The media frenzy reached a fever pitch, each report a grim reminder of the city's vulnerability. The Son of Sam had not just killed individuals; he had assaulted the very spirit of New York, leaving an indelible mark of fear and loss.

Behind the Madness

The mind of David Berkowitz, a labyrinth of twisted thoughts and dark impulses, remains a subject of macabre fascination. In the depths of his psyche, the seeds of violence germinated early, nurtured by a childhood marred by abandonment and confusion. His discovery of his adoption and birth circumstances unleashed a torrent of emotions, a destabilizing force that fractured his already fragile sense of self. Forensic anthropologists would later pinpoint this moment as the catalyst for his descent into infamy.

In the army, Berkowitz found a semblance of structure but not the peace he sought. The discipline and rigor of military life did little to quell the turmoil within. His return to civilian life marked the beginning of a downward spiral, his inner chaos manifesting in a series of nondescript jobs, each a temporary anchor in a sea of internal unrest. His interactions with his biological mother, rather than offering closure, only intensified his sense of alienation and rejection.

The transformation from a troubled individual to a notorious serial killer was marked by an escalation in violence. His early criminal activities, petty and largely unnoticed, evolved into acts of arson and ultimately culminated in murder. The switch from a knife to a gun marked a chilling progression in his methodology, an embrace of a more impersonal, yet more lethal means of expressing his inner demons.

The .44 caliber Bulldog revolver became an extension of his twisted psyche, a tool to externalize the rage and confusion festering within. Each attack, random yet calculated, was a reflection of his fragmented mind, seeking out victims who bore the superficial traits he had come to loathe. The dark streets of New York became his canvas, on which he painted a tapestry of terror and bloodshed, each shooting a grotesque masterpiece of his inner turmoil.

His taunting letters to the police and media were the cries of a man lost in his own madness, seeking recognition and perhaps understanding in a world he felt profoundly disconnected from. These communications, a mix of boasting and cryptic references, were a window into his disordered mind, a mind that reveled in the chaos and fear he had sown. In the end, Berkowitz's legacy is not just the lives he took or the fear he instilled, but the unsettling glimpse he offered into the depths of human depravity.

Letters to the Police: Taunting Authorities

The city's fear was amplified by Berkowitz's macabre communication with the authorities. His letters, a disturbing blend of taunts and riddles, added a psychological dimension to his reign of terror. Each missive was a window into his twisted psyche, revealing a man who reveled in the chaos he had created. The first letter, discovered at a crime scene, introduced the world to the self-styled 'Son of Sam,' a moniker that would become synonymous with unbridled evil. Its block capitals screamed off the page, each word a testament to his deranged state of mind.

His correspondence with Daily News columnist Jimmy Breslin marked a chilling escalation in his game of cat and mouse with the police. The letter, sophisticated in its wording and presentation, was a stark contrast to the crude violence of his physical attacks. It spoke of a man who was not just content with physical violence but sought to invade the minds and living rooms of an entire city. The taunts directed at Breslin were not just threats but a perverse form of outreach, seeking validation in the public eye.

The letters served not only to taunt but to terrorize. They turned the public into unwilling participants in his sadistic saga. Women in New York, already living in fear of being the next victim, now had to contend with the knowledge that the killer was communicating, almost gloating, about his deeds. The letters transformed Berkowitz from a faceless menace into a sinister presence lurking in the collective consciousness of the city.

The police, already under immense pressure to capture the Son of Sam, found themselves deciphering cryptic messages filled with biblical references and bizarre claims. Each new letter was a puzzle piece in an unsolvable puzzle, a sadistic clue left by a killer who seemed to be always one step ahead. The letters did more than taunt; they mocked the efforts of the police, underscoring their impotence in the face of such brazen evil.

The media's role in disseminating the content of these letters added another layer of terror. The press, voracious for details and eager to satisfy the public's hunger for information, became an unwitting accomplice in Berkowitz's psychological warfare. Each published letter amplified the killer's voice, his words reverberating through the city's streets and alleys, a constant reminder of the terror that had gripped New York. The letters were not just messages; they were weapons in themselves, wielded with malicious intent to spread fear and despair.

The Final Summer: 1977's Reign of Terror

The summer of 1977 was sweltering, the city's streets simmering under the relentless sun, an ominous prelude to the horror that would unfold. In the early hours of July 31st, the tranquility of Bath Beach was shattered. Stacy Moskowitz and Robert Violante, enveloped in the innocence of a first date, became the final prey in the Son of Sam's blood-soaked saga. The night's gentle breeze turned acrid with gunpowder as Berkowitz approached. Four shots rang out, their echoes carving a permanent scar in the city's memory. Moskowitz, her life snuffed out, became a symbol of the stolen youth and innocence, while Violante, robbed of his sight, bore the lifelong scars of that night's savagery.

Days before, the city had been on edge, the first anniversary of the initial .44 caliber shootings looming like a specter. Women chopped off their long, dark hair, a desperate attempt to evade the killer's gaze. The streets, usually teeming with life, were now haunted by an eerie silence. The police, desperate to end the nightmare, had cast a wide net, their efforts a tangible manifestation of the city's palpable fear.

In Yonkers, the mundane act of a patrol officer ticketing Berkowitz's car, parked near a fire hydrant, became the linchpin in unraveling the mystery. Local resident Cacilia Davis's observance of Berkowitz, his car's details, and her subsequent report to the police marked the beginning of the end. The police's methodical investigation led them to Berkowitz's doorstep, the anticipation and dread palpable as they prepared to confront the phantom that had haunted New York for over a year.

The capture was anticlimactic, a stark contrast to the chaos he had unleashed. Berkowitz's calm declaration, "Well, you got me," was a chilling acknowledgment of his guilt. The detectives, expecting resistance or perhaps a final, violent outburst, were met instead with his eerie calmness. His capture not only marked the end of his reign of terror but also the beginning of a city's long journey to healing and understanding.

In the aftermath, the city breathed a collective sigh of relief, yet the scars remained. The Son of Sam laws emerged, a testament to the societal impact of Berkowitz's crimes. The city, forever changed, would remember the summer of 1977 not for its sunlit days but for the darkness that had descended upon it. Berkowitz, in his twisted quest for notoriety, had etched his name into the annals of criminal infamy, leaving behind a legacy of fear, loss, and an enduring question: why?

An Ordinary Childhood?

The early life of David Berkowitz, though seemingly ordinary, was a prelude to the darkness that would later engulf him. Born Richard David Falco, his existence began amidst turmoil. His biological mother's decision to give him away just days after his birth sowed the first seeds of abandonment in his young mind. Adopted by Pearl and Nathan Berkowitz, he grew up in the Bronx, a child seemingly like any other, yet beneath the surface lurked undercurrents of unrest.

Berkowitz's childhood was punctuated by troubling behaviors. His fascination with petty larceny and fire-setting hinted at a deeper malaise. Head injuries sustained during these formative years further complicated his psychological profile. Neighbors and relatives remembered him as difficult and spoiled, a child who often bullied others. His adoptive parents, concerned by his actions, sought the help of a psychotherapist, a testament to the turmoil brewing within him.

The death of his adoptive mother from breast cancer was a turning point. At the vulnerable age of 14, Berkowitz faced another profound loss. The subsequent strain in his relationship with his adoptive father, particularly after his father's remarriage, deepened his sense of isolation. This period marked the beginning of his descent into a world of darkness and confusion, a journey that would eventually lead him down a path of infamy.

Berkowitz's high school years were unremarkable academically, but socially, he remained an outcast, his inner demons growing more pronounced. His graduation in 1971 and subsequent enlistment in the United States Army offered a temporary escape but did little to quell his inner turmoil. His service in South Korea and honorable discharge in 1974 did not provide the stability he desperately needed. Instead, it was during this time that the first signs of his future violent tendencies began to manifest.

The revelation of his adoption and the discovery of his biological mother further unraveled Berkowitz's already fragile psyche. The reunion with his birth mother brought more questions than answers, exacerbating his feelings of rejection and loss of identity. This emotional upheaval set the stage for the horrific acts that would later shock and paralyze New York City. Berkowitz's journey from a troubled child to one of America's most notorious serial killers was marked by a series of unresolved traumas and an unquenchable thirst for something he could never seem to find: a sense of belonging.

C: *Richard Cottingham*

Cottingham's Early Life: A Hidden Darkness

Under the dim glow of neon lights, the streets of 1970s Times Square thrummed with an undercurrent of danger. Here, the predator found his hunting ground, his gaze fixed on the vulnerable. The killer, a seemingly ordinary man by day, transformed under the cover of night. His methods were meticulous, his intent sinister. Women, often young and unsuspecting, fell into his trap, lured by a facade of normalcy.

In secluded rooms, the true horror began. Bound and helpless, the victims faced unspeakable torment. The killer's fascination with bondage turned brutal, his actions driven by a chilling need for control and domination. He inflicted pain with a cold precision, a horrifying blend of torture and psychological terror. Each scream, each plea, seemed only to fuel his twisted desires.

The aftermath revealed a grotesque tableau. Bodies, mutilated beyond recognition, lay discarded. The absence of heads or hands, a signature of his savagery, left authorities grappling with a mystery steeped in brutality. Scenes of carnage, where flames consumed flesh, pointed to a killer devoid of humanity, reveling in the destruction he wrought.

In the quiet aftermath, a sinister collection emerged from the shadows. Trophies, personal items of the victims, kept as macabre mementos. Each piece, a haunting reminder of a life violently ended. These objects, once symbols of individuality and life, now served as chilling tokens of death.

As the city slept, unaware and uneasy, the killer vanished into the night, his identity shrouded in darkness. The streets of Times Square, once bustling with life, now echoed with the whispers of his crimes, a lingering testament to the horror that had unfolded in their midst.

The Torso Murders: Gruesome Discoveries

The streets of New York in the 1970s, a melting pot of the unnoticed and the nefarious, became the hunting ground for a relentless predator. Amidst the neon-lit haze, he prowled, his outward normalcy a deceitful mask. The killer, by day a face in the crowd, transformed as darkness fell, driven by a macabre fascination with the suffering of others.

In hidden rooms, the horror unfolded. His victims, unsuspecting and vulnerable, were subjected to unspeakable acts. Bound and defenseless, they were at the mercy of a mind warped by sadistic desires. He reveled in their pain, their fear fueling his twisted appetite for control. The brutality of his methods, a grotesque dance of torture and terror, left a chilling signature.

The aftermath of his deeds painted a scene of unrelenting horror. Bodies, mutilated and unrecognizable, were discovered in desolate places, stripped of identity and humanity. He left a trail of blood and ashes, his victims' remains a testament to his cruel indulgence. The absence of defining features on the bodies pointed to a methodical, monstrous intent.

In the shadows of his private world, he harbored grim trophies. Personal items from his victims, souvenirs of his violence, lay concealed, each a silent witness to a life violently extinguished. These remnants, once cherished possessions, now served as macabre reminders of the terror that had befallen their owners.

The city, oblivious to the monster in its midst, continued its restless rhythm. But beneath the surface, a palpable fear lingered, a community haunted by the unspeakable acts that had violated its streets. The killer, his identity shrouded in darkness, faded into the night, leaving behind a legacy of fear and a series of crimes that would long echo in the annals of true crime.

A Trail of Sorrow: Victims of The Torso Killer

Amid the shadowy corners of a city plagued by vice and secrecy, a monster roamed, blending seamlessly into the crowd. His eyes, cold and calculating, scoured the streets for prey, drawn to the vulnerable and the overlooked. By day, he was just another face in the bustling throngs of the city, his true nature cloaked beneath a veneer of normalcy.

In the solitude of hidden rooms, his dark desires came to life. Here, he orchestrated a symphony of terror, reveling in the control he wielded over his captives. The air was thick with the scent of fear and pain, as he indulged in his grotesque fantasies. His victims, rendered powerless, were subjected to unspeakable acts of violence and degradation, their pleas for mercy falling on deaf ears.

The aftermath of his cruelty lay bare in the cold light of day. Bodies, brutalized and discarded, told a tale of inhumanity and savagery. His signature was unmistakable - a gruesome disfigurement, a macabre trademark of his reign of terror. The lifeless forms, once vibrant and full of promise, now bore the scars of his malevolence, their final moments marked by unthinkable agony.

Within the confines of his lair, he hoarded trophies of his conquests - tokens of his twisted triumphs. Each item, a haunting reminder of a life snatched away, served as a perverse memento of his power. These relics, hidden from the world, whispered of the darkness that lurked within him, a sinister reflection of his depraved soul.

As dawn broke, the city awoke, oblivious to the horror that had unfolded in its midst. The killer, his thirst for violence temporarily quenched, retreated into the shadows, his identity shrouded in mystery. The streets, once bustling with life, now echoed with the silent screams of his victims, their stories etched into the annals of the city's darkest chapters.

In His Own Words: Confessions of a Killer

In the underbelly of a city plagued by shadows, a sinister figure lurked, his presence a harbinger of dread. The streets, alive with the pulse of the unsuspecting, served as his hunting ground. He moved with a predator's precision, his gaze fixated on those least likely to be missed. By day, he was a ghost in the crowd, his monstrous nature cloaked in an unremarkable facade.

In the confines of his secret domain, a chamber of horrors unfolded. Here, he played the role of a merciless tormentor, his hands instruments of unfathomable cruelty. His victims, ensnared in his web, faced agonies that defied comprehension. Their cries echoed in the dank air, a chorus of despair and helplessness.

The aftermath of his brutality was a tableau of terror. The victims, their bodies bearing the scars of unspeakable savagery, lay in silent accusation. He left a signature of horror upon them, a gruesome testament to his perverse desires. The scenes of his crimes, steeped in violence, whispered of the darkness that had descended upon them.

In the stillness of his lair, he surrounded himself with macabre souvenirs. Each item, a grim token of his conquests, stood as a testament to his reign of terror. These chilling trophies, shrouded in secrecy, were the remnants of lives violently stolen, echoes of screams that had long since faded.

As dawn broke, casting light upon the city's façade of normalcy, the predator vanished into the shadows. The streets, once scenes of unspeakable horror, resumed their daily rhythm, oblivious to the nightmares that had unfolded within. The killer, a phantom in the daylight, left behind a legacy of fear and suffering, etched forever in the city's hidden history.

Cottingham's Psychopathy

In the heart of a city teeming with life, a shadow moved with sinister intent. The streets, a maze of potential and peril, were his hunting ground. He blended into the urban tapestry, his monstrous nature masked by the mundane. His eyes, cold and calculating, scanned for the vulnerable, the forgotten.

Behind closed doors, his true self emerged, a fiendish architect of terror. His lair, a grotesque arena where innocence met its end. Bound and helpless, his victims faced an onslaught of unspeakable horrors. Their cries, muffled and desperate, reverberated against the walls, a haunting soundtrack to their plight.

In the aftermath, a chilling silence fell. The scenes he left behind were macabre displays of his brutality. Bodies, mutilated and defiled, lay in a grotesque mockery of rest. His signature was a ghastly imprint of savagery, a testament to his perverse desires. Each crime scene was a frozen moment of terror, a gruesome snapshot of his dark craft.

Amidst the chaos of his abhorrent acts, he collected ghastly mementos. Personal items of his victims, tokens of his conquests, were hidden away in his den of horrors. These relics, once symbols of life and joy, now served as morbid reminders of the souls he had stolen.

As dawn crept over the city, the monster receded into the shadows. The streets, unaware of the nightmare that had unfolded, continued their rhythmic pulse. But for those touched by the horror, the city's heartbeat was forever altered, echoing with the unspeakable acts that had transpired in its darkest corners.

D: *Jeffrey **D**ahmer*

Dahmer's Troubled Adolescence

In the dimly lit corridors of the mind, where shadows whisper secrets too horrific to bear, the story of a predator emerges, not from the wild, but from the very streets we walk. This monster, a seemingly ordinary man, harbored a darkness so profound that it swallowed souls whole. Blood, a constant reminder of his deeds, stained his hands as he meticulously dissected his prey. The scent of death lingered, a morbid perfume, in the air of his abode, mingling with the stench of decay. Each corner of his lair was a testament to the grotesque tableau of his mind, a mind that viewed humans not as beings but as objects to fulfill his macabre fantasies.

His victims, once vibrant and full of life, lay motionless, their final screams echoing in the void of his conscience. Eyes that once held dreams and aspirations now stared blankly, void of the spark that signifies life. The killer's tools, sinister extensions of his will, lay neatly arranged, each one with its own story of terror. These instruments of death, coated with the crimson life force of those he claimed, were not just tools but trophies, symbols of his control over life and death.

In the dead of night, when the world sleeps blissfully unaware, he hunted, driven by an insatiable hunger that no moral compass could deter. The city, a hunting ground, teemed with unsuspecting prey, each potential victim a pawn in his twisted game. His methodical approach was chilling, each step calculated to inflict maximum terror. The chase, a dance with death, where he led and they inevitably followed, was his addiction. The fear in their eyes, a fleeting glimpse into the abyss of his soul, fueled his depraved desires.

The aftermath of his feasts was a scene of unimaginable horror, human forms stripped of dignity and reduced to mere shells. Entrails, once hidden within the sanctity of the body, were exposed to the cold air, a gruesome spectacle of his dominion over flesh. The blood, a river of life, now stood still, a stark red against the pale canvas of death. His signature, a macabre arrangement of the remains, left a message to the world, a declaration of his power and the futility of resistance.

Yet, amidst the carnage, a sinister satisfaction lurked within him, a twisted sense of accomplishment. Each life taken was a piece added to his collection, a distorted gallery of his making. But as the dawn broke, casting light on the night's atrocities, it also brought the inevitable closing of the curtain on this ghastly performance. The monster, now a mere man, retreated into the shadows, waiting, yearning for the night to fall again, for the hunt to begin anew, and for the story of terror to be etched once more in the annals of the damned.

The Milwaukee Murders: A Chilling Chronology

Under the cloak of darkness, a figure lurks, his footsteps silent as the grave. The city sleeps, unaware of the predator in their midst, a human-shaped void with a soul as black as the night. His eyes, cold and unfeeling, scan the streets, hunting for his next victim. With each heartbeat, his anticipation grows, a crescendo of bloodlust that drowns out any semblance of humanity. His hands, instruments of death, itch with the desire to feel the warm blood of another life slipping through his fingers.

The chosen one walks alone, their steps echoing in the silent street, oblivious to the fate that shadows them. A sudden rustle, a whisper of movement, and then the strike. The predator pounces, his strength overwhelming, his grip iron. Panic flutters in the victim's eyes, a dawning realization of the nightmare they've stepped into. The struggle is brief, the outcome never in doubt. The city's symphony plays on, indifferent to the muffled cries that fade into the night.

In the aftermath, the scene is a grotesque masterpiece of his making. The alleyway, a canvas of concrete and trash, now bears the crimson splatter of life violently taken. The body, once a vessel of dreams and laughter, lies broken, the final expression one of terror. The air is thick with the scent of iron and fear, a pungent reminder of the brutality of the act. He stands over his work, admiring the chaos wrought by his hands, the silence now a companion to his dark satisfaction.

As dawn breaks, the city stirs, blissfully ignorant of the horror that unfolded in the shadows. The alleyway, a crime scene swarming with blue uniforms and flashing lights, tells a story of unspeakable violence. The investigators move meticulously, collecting evidence, piecing together the narrative of the night's events. The whispers start, a wave of fear that ripples through the community. Another has fallen prey to the beast that walks among them, a specter of death that vanishes with the morning light.

Yet, even as the city recoils in horror, the predator watches, his hunger undiminished. The thrill of the hunt, the ecstasy of the kill, it's an addiction, a craving that can never be sated. He blends back into the crowd, just another face, his monstrous nature cloaked in mundane normalcy. The game continues, the streets his playground, and the people his unwitting pawns. The cycle of predator and prey spins on, a dance of death that only ends when the final curtain falls, leaving behind a legacy of fear and blood.

Inside Dahmer's Lair: Grisly Evidence

Shadows crept along the walls of the narrow alley as he watched, waiting with a predator's patience. His mind, a twisted labyrinth of dark desires, fixated on the act to come. The city, alive with the hum of the unsuspecting, provided the perfect backdrop for his sinister symphony. Each step he took was deliberate, a silent promise of the terror he was about to unleash. The anticipation hung heavy in the air, a palpable force that drove him forward into the night.

The victim, a solitary figure cutting through the darkness, became the focus of his intense gaze. Unaware of the danger lurking just steps behind, they continued, their fate sealed by his unyielding resolve. In one swift motion, he struck, the sound of struggle abruptly slicing through the stillness. The dance of death unfolded in the shadows, a brutal ballet of predator and prey. His grip tightened, the life beneath his hands fading, a perverse satisfaction swelling within him with each passing moment.

In the aftermath, the alley bore witness to the savagery of man. Blood, a stark contrast against the grimy pavement, painted a picture of the struggle that had ensued. The body, now void of life, lay in a twisted heap, discarded as if it were nothing more than refuse. He lingered, surveying his handiwork, the scent of death mingling with the acrid stench of the city. This place, once an anonymous passageway, had transformed into a macabre stage for his gruesome performance.

As the first light of dawn began to pierce the night, the city awoke, oblivious to the nightmare that had unfolded in its heart. The discovery of the body sent shockwaves through the streets, a community grappling with the reality of the monster in their midst. The crime scene buzzed with activity, each officer and investigator a player in a scenario that had become all too familiar. The echoes of the night's horror reverberated through the alleys and avenues, a grim reminder of the darkness that dwelled within.

He watched from a distance, the chaos he'd created unfolding before his eyes. The fear, the sorrow, the outrage—they were the chorus to his twisted tune. As the city mourned, he reveled in the aftermath, the power he wielded through terror an intoxicating force. But even as they searched, he vanished into the crowd, his presence erased by the very ordinariness that cloaked him. The streets, once a place of connection and life, had become his hunting ground, the stage for a tale of horror that was far from over.

Public Reaction and Media Circus

As night descended, a chilling silence enveloped the streets, a prelude to the macabre performance about to unfold. He moved through the darkness, a specter of death, his every step measured, his every breath a whisper of impending doom. The city, a vast stage set for his sinister act, lay unsuspecting, its inhabitants mere characters in a narrative they hadn't chosen. His mind, a vortex of twisted fantasies, was poised to etch another tale of terror into the annals of the night.

The unsuspecting victim, a lone soul wandering the labyrinth of city streets, became the unwitting star of his dreadful drama. As they meandered, lost in thought, the shadow of fate loomed large, a dark crescendo building with each heartbeat. He watched, waited, and then, with the precision of a maestro conducting a symphony of screams, he struck. The air, once filled with the mundane murmurs of life, now resonated with a guttural symphony of struggle and despair.

The aftermath was a scene pulled from the deepest recesses of nightmare. The ground, a canvas of concrete, bore the gruesome brushstrokes of the struggle that had taken place. Blood, a vibrant crimson, narrated a story of savagery and loss, its every drop a word in the language of horror. He stood amidst the chaos, a conductor surveying the orchestra of pain he had orchestrated, the life he had extinguished reduced to a mere prop in his grotesque tableau.

Dawn's first light brought with it the harsh reality of the night's events. The body, a macabre artifact of human depravity, lay exposed, a silent testament to the fragility of life. The city, now awake, recoiled in horror at the brutality unveiled in its midst. Blue uniforms swarmed the scene, a flurry of activity in a desperate attempt to piece together the narrative of the night. Yet, amidst the search for answers, the palpable sense of dread lingered, a community held hostage by the fear of the unknown.

He watched from the shadows, his identity shrouded in the ordinariness that surrounded him. The chaos, the fear, the relentless pursuit—it all unfolded exactly as he had anticipated. He was an artist of death, and the city, his gallery, displayed his works in all their morbid glory. As the day progressed, he disappeared into the sea of faces, his existence a secret hidden in plain sight. The streets, once a haven of life and light, had become the backdrop for his dark symphony, a melody of murder that played on in the minds of all who dared to remember.

Dissecting Dahmer: A Clinical Viewpoint

The city's underbelly, a labyrinth of darkened alleys and desolate streets, became his hunting ground as the moon cast its pallid glow. There, he prowled, a phantom amongst shadows, his presence an omen of the carnage to come. Each step was a silent vow of violence, a pledge to satiate the ravenous beast that dwelled within his twisted psyche. The air, thick with the anticipation of the hunt, quivered as if aware of the atrocity it was about to witness.

A solitary figure, lost in the embrace of the night, wandered into his sinister web. Oblivious to the eyes that tracked their every move, they continued, their fate sealed by his unyielding intent. In one swift, merciless act, the predator revealed himself, his actions a brutal ballet of ferocity and control. The struggle was brief yet savage, a desperate dance between life and its impending end. The screams that pierced the night sky were a morbid aria to his ears, the sound of life ebbing away the only melody he cherished.

The aftermath painted a portrait of unbridled horror. The ground, once indifferent, now bore the stains of a life stolen, the crimson evidence a stark testament to the ferocity of human cruelty. There, amidst the detritus of the city, lay the remnants of existence, a body now devoid of the spirit it once housed. He lingered, a spectator to the tragedy he authored, the scent of blood a sweet perfume that filled his senses with a grotesque delight.

As dawn broke, casting light upon the hidden corners of the city, the horror of the night's events began to unfurl. The discovery of the body sent ripples of terror through the heart of the community, a stark reminder of the monster that walked among them. Detectives and forensic teams descended upon the scene, a flurry of activity in the grim theatre of death. The city awoke to a nightmare made real, the safety once taken for granted shattered by the brutality of the act.

Yet, even as the city reeled from the shock, he watched, an anonymous figure in the crowd. The chaos, the mourning, the fear—they were the fruits of his labor, a twisted confirmation of his power over life and death. As the city searched for the monster behind the mask, he walked free, his dark deeds a secret cloaked in the mundane. The streets, a stage for his macabre performance, awaited his return, for his thirst for the chase, the fear, and the blood was far from quenched. The symphony of horror was his to conduct, and the city, his unwilling orchestra, played on.

E: *Elias Abuelazam*

The Slasher's Beginning

In the dimly lit streets of a quiet town, a shadowy figure emerged, blending into the night. His steps were measured, his gaze predatory, scanning for unsuspecting victims. This man, a seemingly ordinary individual, harbored a gruesome secret. Under the cover of darkness, he approached his targets, feigning innocence and need. Yet, within moments, the facade crumbled, revealing his true intent. With a swift, violent motion, he unleashed his fury, his knife plunging deep into flesh. The air was filled with the sounds of struggle, the desperate gasps of his victims clashing with his cold, calculated silence.

In this eerie setting, the slasher's reign of terror began. Each attack was a meticulously orchestrated spectacle of horror. The streets, once safe havens, transformed into stages for his sadistic performances. With each strike, he carved a path of fear and bloodshed, leaving behind a trail of pain and unanswered questions. The community, unaware of the lurking danger, continued its nightly routines, unknowingly playing into his hands.

As the nights progressed, the intensity of his assaults escalated. The once sporadic incidents became a hauntingly regular occurrence. Panic started to grip the town, the realization of a serial attacker among them setting in. His victims, chosen at random, were united by the brutality they endured. Their wounds, deep and life-threatening, were not just physical scars, but symbols of the slasher's deep-seated hatred and disregard for human life.

The authorities, initially baffled by the sudden spike in violence, began to connect the dots. Patterns emerged, pointing to a single, ruthless individual. The hunt for the slasher intensified, but he remained elusive, always one step ahead. His understanding of the town's layout and routines allowed him to strike with precision, leaving little evidence behind.

This chapter in the town's history was marked by fear, the residents haunted by the knowledge that one of their own was a monster in disguise. The slasher's beginnings were shrouded in mystery, his motives unknown, but his impact was undeniable. He had instilled a deep, pervasive fear, a reminder of the darkness that can hide beneath the surface of any community.

Shadows in Flint: A Pattern Emerges

In the depths of Flint's urban sprawl, a horrifying pattern began to unfold, painting a nightmarish scene in the once peaceful city. Under the cloak of darkness, the streets became a hunting ground for a predator, whose appetite for violence knew no bounds. His victims, chosen indiscriminately, were left in a state of terror and disbelief, their wounds speaking volumes of the brutality they endured. The city's nights were pierced by the echoes of his savagery, turning every alley and corner into a potential death trap.

As the series of attacks continued, a sense of dread enveloped Flint. The community, once vibrant and bustling, now found itself grappling with the reality of a lurking menace. The assailant moved like a phantom through the streets, his presence felt yet unseen, his identity a mystery. With each attack, he left behind a signature of cruelty, a gruesome reminder of his existence. The wounds inflicted were not just physical but emotional, tearing at the fabric of the community.

Investigations into these heinous crimes became a top priority for law enforcement. The pattern of the attacks offered clues but also raised unsettling questions about the motive and identity of the perpetrator. Was this the work of a lone wolf, a deranged individual driven by some unfathomable desire? Or was it a more calculated campaign of terror, designed to instill fear and chaos? The answers seemed to slip further away with each passing night.

The community's resilience was put to the test as the shadow of fear grew longer with each incident. Vigilance became a way of life, the simple act of stepping outside fraught with anxiety and suspicion. Parents clutched their children a little tighter, and neighbors looked upon one another with a mix of fear and uncertainty. The once familiar streets of Flint had transformed into a macabre stage where an unknown terror played the lead role.

As the city reeled from the impact of these brutal assaults, a collective resolve began to form. The people of Flint, bound by their shared ordeal, started to come together, their determination to reclaim their city from the clutches of this unknown assailant growing stronger. In the face of adversity, Flint's spirit of community shone through, a beacon of hope amidst the darkness that had descended upon the city.

A Trail of Terror: Cross-Country Escapades

The serial killer's reign of terror was not confined to a single town; it was a malignant journey that spanned across states. In these cross-country escapades, he left behind a gruesome tapestry of violence and fear. Each location bore the scars of his mercilessness, with scenes marked by haphazard splatters of blood and the desolate cries of his victims echoing in the still night air. His method of operation was chillingly consistent: a sudden, brutal ambush, unleashing a barrage of stabs that tore through flesh and bone. The randomness of his attacks sowed a deep-seated terror, rendering every shadow a potential harbinger of death.

The predator's bloodlust drove him beyond the familiar streets of Flint to unsuspecting towns where his presence lurked like an unseen specter. In each new setting, he adapted with a disturbing ease, his guise of normalcy masking the monster within. His victims, chosen without discernible pattern, found themselves ensnared in his twisted game, their final moments a frenzied struggle against a relentless assailant. The aftermath of each attack left communities reeling, grappling with the reality of the horror that had visited them.

With each new location, law enforcement scrambled to piece together the fragmented puzzle of his identity. Yet, he remained a step ahead, his enigmatic nature clouding their efforts. The trail he left was a dizzying array of clues, but they seemed to lead only to more questions, more dead ends. It was as if he reveled in the chaos he wrought, his every move calculated to confound and terrorize.

As the body count rose, so did the urgency to apprehend this nomadic fiend. The pressure mounted on law enforcement agencies, each new crime scene a grim reminder of their race against time. The public's fear escalated with each report of his atrocities, their collective anxiety palpable. He had become a ghostly figure, his identity shrouded in mystery, his motives as elusive as his shadowy form.

In the wake of his violence, survivors were left to bear the scars, both physical and emotional. Their accounts painted a haunting picture of their encounters with the killer, each story a fragmented piece of a larger, more horrifying image. The agony etched on their faces, the tremor in their voices, bore witness to the depth of their trauma. They were the ones who had stared into the abyss and survived, their lives forever altered by the brush with pure evil.

Capture and Confession

In a dramatic turn of events, the elusive phantom that had haunted city streets was finally ensnared. His capture, not in the dark alleys of Flint but in the bustling corridors of an Atlanta airport, marked a climactic end to a nationwide manhunt. As he stood there, the reality of his impending fate written across his face, the magnitude of his reign of terror began to unravel. This moment of capture was more than just the apprehension of a fugitive; it was the culmination of fear, anxiety, and relentless pursuit.

In the interrogation room, under the stark, unyielding glare of the lights, he began to unravel the ghastly tapestry of his crimes. Each confession peeled back layers of horror, revealing the depths of his depravity. The words spilled from him, a macabre litany of places, dates, and brutal acts. It was not just a recounting of his heinous deeds; it was an admission of a mind twisted by an insatiable bloodlust. The air in the room grew heavy with the weight of his words, each sentence a chilling reminder of the lives he had shattered.

His confessions were punctuated by a chilling lack of remorse, his voice steady, almost detached. It was as if he were narrating someone else's story, not the gruesome reality of his own making. The details were vivid and unflinching, painting a picture of a man who viewed his victims not as humans, but as mere objects in his twisted game. This detachment only added to the horror, his indifference to the suffering he caused as chilling as the acts themselves.

As the scale of his crimes became apparent, a collective shudder ran through the communities he had terrorized. The relief of his capture was tempered by the haunting knowledge of what he had done. Families of victims, law enforcement, and the public alike struggled to comprehend the enormity of his actions. His confession brought closure to some, but for many, it opened deep wounds that might never fully heal.

In the aftermath of his confessions, a picture began to emerge of a man who had walked among us, hidden in plain sight. His story was a stark reminder of the darkness that can lurk beneath the surface of the ordinary, a testament to the unfathomable depths of human depravity. His words, cold and unyielding, left an indelible mark on the psyche of a nation, a grim legacy of a mind consumed by violence.

Psychological Underpinnings

In the cold, sterile environment of a psychiatric evaluation room, experts delved into the psyche of the man behind the bloodshed. His mind, a labyrinthine web of darkness and distortion, became the subject of intense scrutiny. The evaluations sought to uncover what drove him to such extremes of violence. Was it a deep-seated pathology, an inherent flaw in his psychological makeup, or something more sinister? His demeanor in these sessions was unnervingly calm, his responses measured, yet beneath this facade lay a chilling truth: a mind driven by impulses so dark, they were almost beyond comprehension.

The debate raged among professionals: was he a victim of his own mind, a pawn in the grip of mental illness, or was he fully aware, reveling in the control and power of his actions? His history painted a complex portrait, one marred by instances of emotional instability and flashes of anger, yet there was no clear trajectory that pointed inevitably to murder. This complexity only deepened the mystery, blurring the lines between madness and calculated malevolence.

In court, his defense hinged on the argument of mental illness, their case built on a foundation of psychiatric testimony and clinical assessments. However, the prosecution's experts painted a starkly different picture. They saw a man who, despite his mental health struggles, possessed a clear understanding of right and wrong, a man who chose to embrace the darkness within him. Their arguments depicted a chilling figure, one who operated not out of compulsion, but out of a deliberate, conscious decision to inflict pain and suffering.

As the jury weighed the evidence, the question of his sanity became a pivotal point in the trial. How much did his mental state contribute to his actions? Could his heinous deeds be fully explained by a disordered mind, or was there an element of inherent evil, a conscious decision to unleash terror upon unsuspecting victims? This dilemma lay at the heart of the trial, a complex interplay of psychology, morality, and law.

In the end, the verdict reflected not just a judgment on his actions, but also a statement on the nature of evil. The conclusion drawn by the court resonated far beyond the confines of the courtroom, sparking debates and discussions about the human capacity for violence. It was a verdict that did not just close a case, but also opened a window into the darkest corners of the human psyche, a glimpse into the abyss of a killer's mind.

F: *George Fitzsimmons*

The Genesis of George Fitzsimmons: An Unsettling Start

In the dimly lit, decrepit house where George Fitzsimmons spent his formative years, shadows seemed to cling to the walls like specters. Here, amid the decay and neglect, a young George's fascination with death took root. His first encounter with mortality was not through a pet or a distant relative, but through his own actions. At the tender age of eight, he dismantled a bird's nest, its fragile occupants tumbling to the ground, their tiny bones cracking under his curious fingers. The incident, seemingly trivial to an onlooker, marked the inception of a macabre curiosity that would define his later years.

His teenage years were characterized by a chilling escalation. He roamed the streets at night, drawn to the alleys and backroads where society's eyes rarely lingered. It was during these nocturnal wanderings that he claimed his first human victim, a homeless man whose disappearance went largely unnoticed. Fitzsimmons, then just 16, experienced an intoxicating rush of power as he watched the life drain from his victim's eyes. The act was not one of passion or anger, but a calculated experiment in control and dominance.

As he matured into adulthood, Fitzsimmons' methods grew more sophisticated, his choices of victims more deliberate. Women, he found, were particularly intriguing subjects. He relished not just the act of killing, but the meticulous planning and stalking that preceded it. Each victim was carefully selected, observed, and ultimately ensnared in a web of calculated terror. He didn't just take lives; he crafted each murder like a piece of macabre art, leaving signature marks that would later haunt the dreams of investigators.

His lair, a secluded cabin in the woods, became a tableau of his twisted fantasies. Here, he kept mementos of his victims: locks of hair, personal items, and in the most disturbing cases, photographs of their final moments. The walls were adorned with chilling sketches and notes, detailing each act in horrifying detail. This macabre sanctuary was where

Fitzsimmons felt most alive, surrounded by the echoes of his gruesome deeds.

Yet, despite the horror he wrought, Fitzsimmons maintained a veneer of normalcy in his day-to-day life. To his neighbors and coworkers, he was unremarkable, just another face in the crowd. This duality was perhaps the most terrifying aspect of his persona. It was a stark reminder that monsters don't always lurk in the shadows; sometimes, they walk among us, cloaked in the guise of the ordinary, waiting for the night to fall and their true nature to emerge.

Fitzsimmons' Reign of Fear: A String of Horrors

The night air was thick with an ominous chill as Fitzsimmons prowled the dimly lit streets, his senses heightened by the thrill of the hunt. His mind, a twisted labyrinth of dark desires, fixated on his next victim. The unsuspecting woman, lost in her thoughts, became the target of his malevolent intentions. He followed her with a predator's patience, every step a silent promise of the horror to come.

In the shadows, he struck with a brutality that was both shocking and deliberate. His hands, instruments of death, wrapped around her throat, squeezing the life from her with a cold, calculated precision. Her struggles were futile against his overpowering strength. As she gasped her final breaths, a twisted satisfaction washed over him. This act was not just a killing; it was an assertion of his dominance over life and death.

The aftermath of the murder was a grotesque scene. The alley, once just a forgotten passage, was transformed into a canvas of his savagery. Her body, lifeless and defiled, lay in a pool of congealing blood, her eyes wide with the terror of her final moments. He took his time, admiring his work, the scent of blood mingling with the cold night air. This was his art, each victim a morbid masterpiece.

As the city slept, unaware of the monster in its midst, Fitzsimmons vanished into the night. His appetite for violence unsated, he was already envisioning his next conquest. The police, baffled and outpaced, could only react to the aftermath of his atrocities. The community, paralyzed by fear, whispered his name with a mix of dread and disbelief. He wasn't just a killer; he was a specter, a ghostly presence that haunted their darkest nightmares.

The legacy of his reign of terror was a tapestry of pain and fear. Families shattered, lives ruined, and a city forever scarred by his actions. Fitzsimmons, in his unyielding pursuit of control and power, had not just taken lives; he had altered the very fabric of countless others. His crimes were a chilling reminder of the depths of human depravity, a dark stain on the pages of history that would never be erased.

The Art of Evasion: Fitzsimmons' Elusive Tactics

In the game of cat and mouse between Fitzsimmons and law enforcement, the predator was always one step ahead. His ability to vanish into the urban landscape, leaving no trace behind, was uncanny. He moved through the city like a ghost, his presence only felt in the chilling aftermath of his deeds. The police, despite their best efforts, found themselves grappling with shadows, the elusive killer always just beyond their reach.

Each crime scene was a testament to his cunning. He left no fingerprints, no DNA, no definitive evidence that could lead back to him. It was as if he had evaporated into thin air after each heinous act. The meticulous planning that went into every murder was evident, the killer always ensuring that his trail would run cold. His understanding of forensic science was disturbingly sophisticated, allowing him to manipulate crime scenes with an artist's touch.

Fitzsimmons thrived in the underbelly of the city, blending in with the faceless crowds. He was acutely aware of surveillance and police tactics, often altering his appearance and patterns to avoid detection. His transient lifestyle, devoid of any meaningful connections or consistent routine, made it nearly impossible for the authorities to predict his next move. He was a phantom, operating on the fringes of society, unseen and unknown.

His interactions with his victims were the only times he revealed himself, but even then, he was a master of disguise. He charmed and lured his victims with a practiced ease, his facade as the charming stranger disarming and deceptive. This ability to transform, to wear different masks for different occasions, was a crucial component of his evasive strategy. He was not just hiding from the law; he was hiding in plain sight, a wolf amongst the sheep.

The frustration within the police force was palpable. Each new crime scene was a grim reminder of their failure to catch him.

Fitzsimmons was not just a killer; he was a shadow that haunted their every step. The city, once a bustling metropolis, now felt like a labyrinthine trap, with the killer lurking around every corner, always watching, always waiting for his next opportunity to strike.

The Downfall: Capture and Revelation

The end of Fitzsimmons' reign of terror began on an unremarkable evening, under the cold gaze of a crescent moon. The city, still reeling from his latest atrocity, bristled with a palpable tension. Little did anyone know, the meticulous killer had made his first and last mistake. A single strand of hair, a minuscule oversight, became the unraveling thread of his carefully woven tapestry of deception.

Detectives, fueled by a relentless drive to bring him to justice, pounced on this newfound evidence with a voracity that matched their quarry's cunning. Forensic analysis, now armed with the latest technological advancements, traced the genetic fingerprint back to Fitzsimmons. The hunter had become the hunted, the invisible now starkly exposed under the harsh light of scrutiny.

The operation to apprehend him was swift and precise, a carefully orchestrated maneuver that left no room for error. As dawn broke, the police descended upon his hideout, a nondescript apartment nestled in the heart of the city. They found him, not as the menacing figure of nightmares, but as a man, cornered and stripped of his power. His capture, devoid of the expected confrontation, was anti-climactic yet deeply satisfying.

In the aftermath, the full extent of his horrific spree came to light. Evidence unearthed from his lair painted a vivid picture of his twisted psyche. Photographs, trophies from his victims, and chilling journals detailed each murder with a cold, methodical precision. The community, once paralyzed by fear, now grappled with the reality of the monster who had lived among them.

His trial was a media frenzy, each revelation more shocking than the last. The man who had once evaded capture with such skill now stood exposed, his crimes laid bare for the world to see. Fitzsimmons, the enigmatic shadow that had terrorized the city, was finally unmasked, his legacy forever etched in the annals of criminal infamy.

Inside Fitzsimmons' Mind: A Clinical Exploration

Delving into the psyche of Fitzsimmons revealed a labyrinth of twisted thoughts and morbid fascinations. Psychologists who studied his case were both horrified and intrigued by the complexity of his mind. He exhibited classic signs of psychopathy: a lack of empathy, manipulative behavior, and a chilling disregard for human life. Yet, there was something uniquely disturbing about the way he relished in the meticulous planning and execution of his crimes.

His childhood, upon examination, provided early indicators of his dark path. Reports of animal cruelty and a fascination with death were red flags that went unnoticed. These early behaviors were not just precursors to violence; they were the foundation of a personality that thrived on control and domination. Fitzsimmons didn't just evolve into a killer; he was molded by a confluence of innate predispositions and environmental factors.

During his incarceration, he displayed a cold, unyielding demeanor in interviews. He spoke of his crimes with a detachment that was unnerving, as if he were discussing a mundane task rather than the taking of human lives. This detachment was a key component of his ability to commit such heinous acts without remorse. He viewed his victims not as people, but as objects in his twisted game.

The insights gleaned from his psychological evaluations painted a portrait of a man driven by a deep-seated need for power. His killings were not impulsive acts of violence but calculated expressions of control. This need for dominance was evident in every aspect of his life, from his interactions with others to the way he meticulously orchestrated each murder. Fitzsimmons' mind was a dark realm where empathy and morality were overshadowed by a singular, overwhelming desire to dominate.

In the end, understanding Fitzsimmons' psyche offered little in the way of consolation to his victims' families. It did, however, provide valuable insights into the workings of a serial killer's mind. His case became a reference point in criminal psychology, a stark reminder of the depths of human depravity and the importance of early intervention in cases of extreme antisocial behavior. Fitzsimmons was not just a chapter in the annals of crime; he was a case study in the darkest corners of the human psyche.

G: *Donald Henry Gaskins*

From Troubled Child to Serial Killer

Beneath the guise of an unassuming man, Gaskins harbored a bloodthirsty nature. His transition from a troubled child to a merciless killer began in the shadows of South Carolina's rural landscapes. His early years were marred by abuse and neglect, shaping a psyche devoid of empathy. Gaskins' childhood, a chaotic blend of violence and deprivation, was the kindling for his later atrocities.

As he matured, his criminal activities escalated in both frequency and severity. The young man's penchant for violence was insatiable, culminating in his first murder—a brutal, calculated act that marked the beginning of a horrific spree. His method was cold and predatory; he lured his victims, unsuspecting and vulnerable, into his deadly grasp.

The coastal highways became his hunting ground. Here, he preyed on hitchhikers, embodying their worst nightmares. Each victim's encounter with Gaskins was a descent into a hellish ordeal. His sadistic urges found expression in unspeakable acts of torture and mutilation. The cruelty he inflicted was methodical, each act a testament to his depraved indifference to human life.

Gaskins' reign of terror left a trail of blood and sorrow. The communities he once roamed were haunted by the echoes of his heinous crimes. His victims, stripped of their dignity and life, were mere objects in his twisted game. The memory of their suffering lingers, a chilling reminder of the monstrous capabilities lurking within a human being.

The capture of this monster was a complex and painstaking endeavor. Law enforcement's relentless pursuit eventually brought him to justice, but the scars he left on the fabric of society remain indelible. Gaskins' story is a stark portrayal of the darkest corners of the human soul, a narrative that continues to horrify and fascinate.

The Hitchhikers' Nightmare

Donald Henry Gaskins, often overlooked in the pantheon of American serial killers, etched his name into the annals of crime in the most horrifying ways imaginable. His life, marred by a tortuous childhood, spiraled into a sequence of increasingly violent crimes. It was on the highways of the American South that Gaskins found his most sinister expression, turning the act of hitchhiking into a gateway to terror.

He sought out his victims with a predator's instinct, each hitchhiker a new opportunity for him to unleash his sadistic impulses. These unwitting victims, often young and vulnerable, were drawn into his web of deception, believing they had found a safe passage. Instead, they were plunged into a nightmare, each one subjected to unspeakable torture. Gaskins relished the control he wielded over his captives, prolonging their agony for his own twisted satisfaction.

His methods were gruesomely inventive, a testament to the depths of his depravity. Stabbings, strangulations, and worse – each act was a macabre experiment in human suffering. The screams of his victims echoed through the secluded spots he chose for these heinous acts, far removed from any hope of rescue. The landscape that once symbolized freedom and adventure was now marred by the hidden horrors of Gaskins' making.

The discovery of his crimes sent shockwaves through the communities he had terrorized. Buried in shallow graves, the remains of his victims told a harrowing tale of his brutality. The magnitude of his violence, once unveiled, left a permanent scar on the collective consciousness of the region.

Yet, in the annals of criminal history, Gaskins remains a shadowy figure, his atrocities eclipsed by other notorious killers. His story, a chilling reminder of the evil that can lurk behind a seemingly ordinary facade, continues to haunt the memory of those who cross the quiet highways of the South.

Gaskins' Evolving Methodology

In the macabre journey of Donald Henry Gaskins, each murder marked an evolution in his sadistic methodology. His early crimes, though brutal, lacked the refinement of his later atrocities. Initially driven by impulsive rage, Gaskins soon developed a more calculated approach, selecting his victims with a predator's precision. This chilling progression revealed a deepening of his depravity and a growing appetite for violence.

His tactics became more sophisticated over time, employing psychological manipulation alongside physical brutality. He no longer relied solely on physical force; instead, he used deceit and charm to ensnare his victims. This shift made him even more dangerous, as he could now lure a broader range of victims into his grasp.

The escalation in his methods was accompanied by an increase in the frequency of his killings. What started as sporadic acts of violence transformed into a continuous spree. This surge in activity suggests not only a growing confidence in his abilities but also an insatiable hunger for the thrill of the kill.

Gaskins' evolving methodology culminated in a series of meticulously planned and executed murders. These final acts were the epitome of his cruelty, demonstrating a complete detachment from any semblance of humanity. His ability to adapt and refine his methods over time makes his story one of the most disturbing chapters in the annals of criminal history.

The legacy of Gaskins' killing spree is a testament to the depths of human depravity. His evolution from a violent offender to a methodical serial killer serves as a dark reminder of the potential for escalation in criminal behavior. His story continues to fascinate and horrify, offering a grim insight into the mind of a serial killer.

Gaskins in Focus: Psychological Analysis

The psychological landscape of Donald Henry Gaskins was a complex web of sociopathy, narcissism, and deep-seated sadism. His criminal behavior and heinous acts provide a case study in extreme antisocial personality disorder. Gaskins exhibited a complete lack of moral responsibility and social conscience, characteristics typical of a sociopath.

His narcissistic tendencies were equally pronounced. Gaskins was excessively preoccupied with personal adequacy, power, prestige, and vanity. This self-absorption was coupled with an inability to recognize the destructive impact of his actions, not only on his victims but also on himself.

Gaskins' psychopathy was evident in his sadistic pleasure derived from inflicting pain and suffering. His crimes were not just acts of violence; they were meticulously planned and executed demonstrations of control and dominance. This behavior is indicative of a psychopath who derives gratification from the act of torture itself.

The combination of these psychological disorders created a perfect storm for his evolution into a serial killer. Gaskins' lack of empathy, grandiose sense of self, and sadistic impulses drove him to commit acts of extreme violence with alarming frequency and brutality.

Understanding the psychological underpinnings of Gaskins' behavior is crucial in comprehending the motivations behind his crimes. His case is a grim reminder of the potential dangers posed by individuals with such severe and untreated mental disorders.

H: *Fritz **H**aarmann*

Haarmann's Early Indications of Violence

In the shadowed streets of early 20th-century Hanover, a young Fritz Haarmann lurked, his presence a dark foreboding of the horrors to come. As a child, his unsettling fascination with blood and death was evident. Slaughterhouses became his playgrounds, where the sharp scent of blood and the guttural cries of dying animals stirred something primal within him. This was more than mere childhood curiosity; it was the brewing of a tempest, a harbinger of the gruesome path he would tread.

The adolescent Haarmann's aggression soon transcended the boundaries of mere fantasy. His early criminal record, peppered with petty thefts and burglaries, was but a veil over a more sinister temperament. Instances of violent outbursts, particularly towards smaller, weaker beings, began to surface. These weren't just adolescent scuffles but an exhibition of a deep-seated brutality, a need to dominate and destroy that was bone deep.

As Haarmann matured, the intensity of his violent impulses only escalated. He found himself drawn to the vulnerable, the unnoticed of society—those whose disappearances wouldn't immediately raise alarms. His method was one of charm and deceit, luring his unsuspecting victims with promises of food, work, or shelter. Once under his spell, they were led not to safety but into the clutches of a burgeoning monster.

The transformation from a man to a remorseless killer was gradual yet inexorable. Haarmann's first kill was not just an act of violence; it was a ritualistic release of his pent-up savagery. He didn't just take lives; he obliterated them, leaving behind a trail of mutilated bodies that were barely recognizable as human. The act of killing became an art for Haarmann, each victim a canvas upon which he expressed his darkest desires.

This sinister journey into depravity wasn't just a descent into madness; it was a meticulous cultivation of a killer's instinct. Haarmann didn't just embrace his inner demons; he nurtured them, allowing them to flourish in the underbelly of Hanover. His early life wasn't just a series of violent incidents; it was the formation of a predator, one that would soon be known as the Butcher of Hanover, whose very name would come to evoke terror in the hearts of the city's residents.

The Butcher of Hanover: Gruesome Acts

In the dimly lit backstreets of Hanover, the Butcher prowled, his hunger for brutality insatiable. The air was thick with dread, as if the city itself sensed the looming terror. With each unsuspecting young man that fell under his charm, a sinister plot was set in motion. They vanished into the night, unaware that they were stepping into the lair of a predator. His home, a macabre workshop, was where innocence met its gruesome end.

The Butcher's method was chillingly methodical. He would win over his victims with a smile, a promise, a glimpse of kindness. But as the door closed behind them, the façade crumbled, revealing the monster within. What followed was a horrific display of savagery, where screams were muffled by the thick, unyielding walls of his domain. Each victim was reduced to nothing more than an object of his twisted desires.

Blood was the Butcher's medium, and flesh his canvas. He dismembered his victims with a precision that was both terrifying and awe-inspiring. Limbs were severed, organs removed, with an almost surgical meticulousness. The remains were then scattered, hidden, or sold, erasing their existence from the world. The streets of Hanover became a grotesque exhibition of his handiwork, a city unknowingly dining on its own lost souls.

Yet, it was not just the physical act of murder that defined the Butcher's reign of terror; it was the psychological torment he inflicted. He thrived on the fear, the helplessness, the despair of his victims in their final moments. Their eyes, wide with terror, reflected a darkness so profound it threatened to swallow everything. This was a man who didn't just kill; he feasted on the very essence of life, leaving behind a void where once there was a human being.

The Butcher of Hanover's legacy was not merely the bodies he left behind, but the shadow he cast over the city. Fear gripped Hanover, a fear so palpable it lingered in the air long after his capture. He was more than a murderer; he was a specter of evil that haunted the city's every alley and home. His acts were not just crimes; they were a dark testament to the depths of human depravity, a reminder of the monster that can reside within the guise of a man.

Victims of the Vampire

The city of Hanover, once bustling and lively, now held an air of solemnity, a community shadowed by the unspeakable horrors wrought by the Vampire of Hanover. His victims, young men in the prime of their lives, had vanished into the night, leaving behind a trail of anguish and unanswered questions. Each disappearance sent ripples of fear through the streets, a collective dread that something profoundly evil was lurking among them.

In the Vampire's clutches, these young men faced a terror beyond comprehension. His lair, a place where the line between life and death blurred, became their final, nightmarish destination. Here, in the grip of a predator, their pleas for mercy fell on deaf ears, their cries echoing in a void of utter desolation. The Vampire relished in their fear, each moment of panic feeding his insatiable thirst for blood and suffering.

The horror of the Vampire's acts lay not just in their brutality, but in the callous disregard for the sanctity of life. He drained his victims of their essence, both physically and metaphorically, leaving behind a husk of what once was a vibrant human being. In his wake lay the remnants of lives cut tragically short, dreams unfulfilled, potentials unmet – a tragedy not just for the victims, but for the world they left behind.

With each life he took, the Vampire wove a tapestry of terror that enveloped Hanover. The city, paralyzed by fear, became a place where trust eroded, and suspicion reigned. Neighbors eyed each other warily, wondering if the monster they feared lived among them, masquerading as one of their own. The Vampire's shadow loomed large, a constant, menacing presence that haunted their every waking moment.

The legacy of the Vampire of Hanover was a city forever changed, a community bound together by shared grief and horror. His reign of terror was a stark reminder of the darkness that can reside within the human soul, a darkness capable of transforming a man into a monster. In the hearts of Hanover's residents, the memory of the Vampire and his victims lingered, a somber testament to the fragility of life and the profound impact one man's cruelty can have on the world.

Haarmann's Arrest and Trial

The apprehension of Fritz Haarmann marked a pivotal moment in Hanover's history, a culmination of dread and desperation. It began on a seemingly ordinary day, yet beneath the city's calm surface, a storm was brewing. Detectives, armed with mounting evidence and public outcry, zeroed in on Haarmann. His arrest wasn't just the capture of a man; it was the netting of a fiend who had long masqueraded as human.

In the interrogation room, the air was thick with tension. Haarmann sat, an enigma, his demeanor oscillating between eerie calm and frenzied agitation. As questions pierced the silence, his façades began to crumble, revealing glimpses of the monster within. His confessions, when they came, were not mere admissions but chilling recollections of his barbaric acts. Each word painted a vivid picture of his gruesome exploits, leaving even the seasoned detectives aghast.

The trial of Fritz Haarmann was a spectacle that captured the nation's attention. The courtroom, packed to the rafters, became a stage for the macabre details of his crimes. Witnesses recounted tales of horror, their voices trembling as they relived the nightmares Haarmann had inflicted. Evidence presented, ghastly in its nature, painted a picture of a man whose cruelty knew no bounds. This was not just a trial; it was an exposition of human depravity.

Throughout the proceedings, Haarmann remained an enigma, his expressions ranging from chilling indifference to flashes of anger. His testimony, when given, was a disturbing insight into the mind of a serial killer. He spoke of his crimes with a detachment that was bone-chilling, his words devoid of any remorse. The courtroom became a window into a soul so dark it seemed almost void of humanity.

Haarmann's conviction brought a sense of closure, yet the scars he left on Hanover and its people were indelible. The trial was more than the conclusion of a legal process; it was a cathartic moment for a city haunted by his shadow. As Haarmann was led away, the collective breath held by Hanover was released, not in triumph, but in somber reflection of the horrors endured and the innocent lives lost to the Butcher of Hanover.

Analyzing Haarmann: Clinical Insights

The enigma of Fritz Haarmann, dissected in the sterile light of clinical analysis, presents a chilling portrait of a serial killer. Psychiatrists and criminologists, delving into his psyche, encountered a labyrinth of twisted thoughts and motivations. His actions, far beyond the realm of normal human behavior, were a mosaic of deep-seated psychopathology and unbridled savagery. Understanding him wasn't just a clinical exercise; it was an exploration into the darkest corners of the human mind.

Haarmann's childhood, marked by trauma and neglect, emerged as a critical piece in the puzzle of his psyche. Experts posited that these early experiences forged a path towards his eventual descent into brutality. His emotional development, stunted and warped, manifested in a lack of empathy and a detachment from societal norms. This wasn't just a troubled upbringing; it was the breeding ground for a predator.

The clinical analysis also highlighted Haarmann's complex relationship with aggression and control. His need to dominate his victims, seen in the methodical nature of his killings, spoke of a deep-rooted desire for power. This wasn't mere violence; it was a ritualistic assertion of dominance, a way to exert control in a life where he often felt powerless. Each act of murder was an exercise in reclaiming a sense of agency, however twisted and perverse.

Haarmann's sexual sadism, a focal point of the analysis, painted a picture of a man driven by dark, primal urges. His acts, intertwined with sexual gratification, were more than expressions of lust; they were integral components of his identity as a killer. The intertwining of violence and sexuality in his psyche created a dangerous cocktail that fueled his murderous spree. His desires were not just deviant; they were a critical lens through which to understand his actions.

In the end, the clinical insights into Fritz Haarmann's mind offered a harrowing glimpse into the nature of evil. The analysis was not just an academic exercise; it was a necessary endeavor to understand the complexities of a mind capable of such heinous acts. Haarmann was more than a serial killer; he was a case study in the extremes of human behavior, a dark testament to the potential for evil that lies within.

J: *Keith Hunter Jesperson*

The Birth of a Happy Face Killer

Under the looming shadows of the Canadian mountains, in a small town cradled by Chilliwack, British Columbia, a child's mind twisted under the weight of familial torment and societal rejection. Keith Hunter Jesperson, whose early life was steeped in the agony of abuse and humiliation, found solace in the macabre. His hands, which would later grow to be the instruments of death, began their cruel journey in the silent suffering of animals. The young Jesperson, isolated and ridiculed, descended into a dark world where the lines between life and pain blurred.

In the suffocating confines of a dysfunctional household, Jesperson's father's harsh discipline and mockery forged a heart void of empathy. His childhood, a tapestry of violence and neglect, became the breeding ground for his morose fascinations. The innocent cries of strangled animals, the rush of power in ending a life, these were his grotesque comforts. With each life he snuffed out in the backwoods of British Columbia, a sinister joy grew within him, a precursor to the monstrous future awaiting.

As a towering adolescent, scorned and nicknamed "Igor," Jesperson's violent tendencies escalated. His brutish strength, a stark contrast to his inner turmoil, became a weapon against those weaker. In the classrooms and playgrounds of Selah, Washington, his anger found release in the battering of unsuspecting peers. With each outburst, the once shy and tormented child transformed into a harbinger of terror, his mind spiraling further into the abyss.

The transition from tortured soul to predator was gradual yet inevitable. Jesperson, now a long-haul truck driver, traversed the lonely roads of America, a nomad with a heart of darkness. His towering frame and unassuming demeanor masked a simmering rage against women, a rage birthed from years of rejection and bitterness. The highways became his hunting ground, the endless miles his accomplice. Women, often living on society's fringes, became his prey, their vulnerability a siren call to his twisted desires.

In the dead of night, under the cloak of anonymity, Jesperson's true self emerged. His victims, drawn into his web of deceit, met their end in the most horrifying manner. Strangled, their last breaths a symphony of terror and desperation, they became the faceless trophies of the Happy Face Killer. The smiley faces he drew, a macabre signature, were his taunts to a world he despised, a chilling reminder of the monster that lurked in the shadows of the open road.

Messages in Smiley: A Killer's Taunt

In the early 1990s, the highways of North America became a stage for a macabre performance. The lead actor: a shadowy figure whose seemingly mundane existence as a long-haul trucker belied the darkness within. He stalked his prey with a predator's patience, selecting vulnerable women who vanished into the night, leaving behind only the echo of their despair.

His method was merciless, a ritual of violence that ended in the cold silence of death. The women's final moments were a horrifying dance with the reaper, as his powerful hands closed around their throats. Strangulation, a method he had perfected since childhood, was his signature, leaving behind lifeless bodies devoid of the breath they once held dear.

The killer's twisted sense of pride led him to a unique form of communication. He began leaving messages for the authorities and the media, his words dripping with the glee of a child sharing a secret. These letters, signed with a smiley face, became his calling card, a sinister symbol of the joy he found in his gruesome work.

Each murder heightened his sense of invincibility, emboldening him to continue his spree. The killer reveled in the fear he instilled, his identity shrouded in mystery as the body count rose. The media, frenzied by the elusive nature of the crimes, hung on every word of his chilling correspondence.

Yet, in his overconfidence lay his downfall. The very letters that were meant to taunt the authorities became the breadcrumbs that led to his capture. The smiley faces, once symbols of his triumph, turned into the ironclad evidence of his guilt, sealing his fate and ending his reign of terror.

Road of Rage: Jesperson's Path

The journey of Keith Hunter Jesperson, the man who would become known as the Happy Face Killer, was marked by a relentless escalation of violence. His early years, shadowed by the brutality of an abusive father and the scorn of peers, were the kindling for the inferno of rage that would later consume him. This towering figure, a man who could easily blend into the background of any truck stop or roadside diner, harbored a tempest of anger within.

His first act of ultimate violence, the murder of Taunja Bennett, was not just a release of pent-up fury but also a discovery of a twisted form of ecstasy. In the stillness of that night, as Bennett's breaths grew shallow under the grip of his large, calloused hands, a monstrous appetite awoke within him. The act of extinguishing a human life, to him, was intoxicating, the power over life and death an addictive elixir.

As he continued his bloody pilgrimage across the highways of America, his method became refined, but no less brutal. Each victim was a testament to his growing confidence, his ability to snuff out a life and vanish into the night. Women, often marginalized by society, became the targets of his wrath, their vulnerability a beacon to his predatory instincts.

The killer's journey was not just a series of crimes; it was a descent into the depths of human depravity. With each life he took, he strayed further from any semblance of humanity, becoming a specter of death lurking on the open road. His truck, a seemingly innocuous vehicle, was in reality a moving tomb, a chariot of doom where he enacted his gruesome rituals.

In this tale of terror, the road itself became an accomplice to his crimes, its sprawling, unending expanse providing the perfect cover for his heinous acts. As each mile passed under the wheels of his truck, the line between man and monster blurred, until all that remained was the Happy Face Killer, a phantom haunting the highways of America.

Confessions of a Long-Haul Killer

In the solitary confines of his truck cab, the killer cultivated a realm of horror. Each victim's encounter began with a deceptive calm, the unsuspecting prey lured into a trap by a seemingly harmless man. The reality, however, was far more sinister. Within the confines of the truck, a nightmarish scenario unfolded, the women subjected to unspeakable acts of violence and depravity. His method was cruel and meticulous, ensuring maximum fear and suffering.

His victims' final moments were a maelstrom of terror and confusion. Bound and helpless, they faced a predator whose pleasure derived from their pain and fear. The truck, a transient dungeon, was filled with the echoing screams and pleas of his victims, sounds that were music to his twisted soul. The outside world remained oblivious, the roar of the engine drowning out the horrors within.

The aftermath of his crimes was a ghastly spectacle. Bodies discarded like broken dolls, devoid of the life and vibrancy they once possessed. The killer left his victims in desolate, forgotten places, their last resting spots as transient as their killer's lifestyle. The stark contrast between the serene landscapes and the violence inflicted upon these women was a testament to the killer's cold, calculated nature.

With each murder, he grew bolder, leaving behind cryptic messages and taunting law enforcement. These communications were not just boasts but part of the game he relished. The killer thrived on the notoriety, the fear he instilled, and the control he exerted even from afar. The media, inadvertently, became a tool for his ego, spreading his infamy and stoking public fear.

The confessions, when they finally came, were a chilling insight into the mind of a monster. His words were devoid of remorse, recounting each act with a detached, almost clinical precision. To the killer, these were not confessions but trophies, a recounting of his macabre achievements. The law's net had tightened, but in his mind, he had already won, immortalized by his heinous acts.

Happy Face Unmasked: Psychological Profile

The psyche of Keith Hunter Jesperson unraveled a chilling narrative of a mind steeped in sadism and devoid of empathy. His early life, marred by abuse and alienation, laid the groundwork for his devolution into a remorseless killer. As a child, the pleasure derived from the suffering of animals was a precursor to his later atrocities. This lack of empathy, a defining characteristic of his psychological profile, manifested in the ultimate dehumanization of his victims.

His crimes were not impulsive acts but carefully orchestrated events, driven by a deep-seated need for power and control. This need was born from a life where he felt powerless and insignificant, only to be realized in the most horrific of ways. His victims, selected for their vulnerability, were mere objects in his twisted game, a means to exert the dominance he so craved.

Jesperson's interactions with his victims exhibited a chilling blend of charm and menace. This duality was a hallmark of his psychopathy, allowing him to mask his true intentions until it was too late. His ability to appear normal, even likable, was a weapon as deadly as any physical tool he used to commit his murders.

The communication of his crimes through letters and confessions was not born of guilt but of ego. These acts were his way of asserting dominance, a continuation of his control even after the act itself. The lack of remorse in these communications was stark, his descriptions clinical, and his pride in his 'work' apparent.

The unraveling of Jesperson's mind offers a harrowing glimpse into the darkness that can reside within a human being. His story is a stark reminder of the depths of depravity to which a person can sink, driven by a twisted psyche unchecked and fueled by a lifetime of anger, resentment, and a desire for control.

K: *Edmund Kemper*

The Co-Ed Butcher: A Trail of Terror

Nightfall draped the Santa Cruz hills in a deceptive tranquility, masking the horrors unfolding beneath its serene veil. The Co-Ed Butcher, a moniker befitting Kemper's gruesome spree, prowled these streets with a predatory gaze. His towering frame, a menacing silhouette against the dim streetlights, belied his soft-spoken demeanor, a ruse that lured unsuspecting victims into his grasp.

Each encounter began innocently enough: an offer of a ride, a friendly smile, the false safety of a gentle giant. But as the car veered into the desolate outskirts of town, the mask would slip, revealing the monster within. His hands, large enough to encircle a neck with ease, became instruments of terror. The young women, plucked from the safety of their mundane lives, were subjected to unspeakable acts. Bound, silenced, their pleas muffled under the weight of his imposing figure, they met their end in a macabre ritual that Kemper perfected with each kill.

The aftermath was a grotesque tableau. In the seclusion of his abode, he dissected his trophies with clinical precision. Severed heads, a chilling testament to his depravity, were arranged in a macabre display of power and perversion. The rest of the bodies, dismembered and desecrated, bore the scars of his unbridled sadism. His actions were not just murders; they were a defilement of humanity, a dark dance with death and depravity.

But Kemper's reign of terror was not limited to strangers. The culmination of his brutality was reserved for the one who ignited his murderous inferno: his own mother. In an act that blurred the lines between vengeance and insanity, he turned his violent impulses towards the woman who had birthed him. The final murder, a grotesque parody of a filial bond severed in blood, marked the peak of his pathological journey.

With the dawn, the nightmare receded into the shadows, leaving behind a trail of grief and unanswered questions. The Co-Ed Butcher had etched his name into the annals of infamy, a dark legacy that lingered long after his capture. His crimes, a stark reminder of the depths of human depravity, left an indelible scar on the collective consciousness of a community forever haunted by the specter of a killer in their midst.

The Co-Ed Butcher: A Trail of Terror

In the shadows of Santa Cruz, a menacing figure lurked, blending into the night. Edmund Kemper, a colossus in stature and horror, embarked on a chilling spree, transforming the quiet streets into a tableau of terror. The unsuspecting victims, young women seeking the freedom of the open road, encountered a fate far darker than the night they vanished into.

He approached with a deceptive gentleness, his hulking form and affable demeanor a mask for the brutality that lay within. As each woman stepped into his car, they crossed an invisible threshold from mundane reality into a nightmare. The journeys, initially mundane, took sinister turns, leading to secluded areas where the true nature of the ride emerged.

Once isolated, Kemper's demeanor shifted, his immense hands and overpowering strength now tools of terror. Each victim's struggle was a futile battle against an overwhelming force, their final moments a cacophony of fear and despair. He transformed their final breaths into a grotesque symphony, a perverse mixture of innocence lost and malevolence unleashed.

Back at his grim sanctuary, Kemper's unspeakable acts continued. The lifeless bodies, now mere objects in his twisted world, underwent a final indignity. Dissection and mutilation were carried out with a chilling precision, his actions painting a picture of a man lost in his own deranged fantasies.

The narrative of the Co-Ed Butcher, a name that would forever echo in the annals of criminal infamy, is a stark reminder of the depths of human depravity. His crimes, etched into the collective memory of a horrified nation, serve as a grim testament to the darkness that can reside within the human soul.

Conversations with a Killer

The blood-curdling saga of Edmund Kemper unravels a tale as harrowing as it is real. In the shadowed streets of Santa Cruz, a predator hunted, his presence a dark omen. Towering at over six feet, he was a looming specter, his outwardly benign demeanor masking a grotesque inner world. His victims, young women embarking on the innocent adventure of hitchhiking, were unwittingly drawn into his web of horror.

Each abduction was a meticulously crafted act, luring victims with the promise of a safe journey. However, once ensnared, the facade crumbled, revealing a monster driven by unspeakable urges. His method was one of cold calculation and barbarity. Bound and helpless, the victims' final moments were a maelstrom of fear, their pleas echoing into the void.

Within the confines of his abode, a macabre ritual unfolded. The stillness of death hung heavy as he engaged in ghastly acts upon the lifeless forms. Dismemberment and desecration were carried out with chilling precision, each action a testament to his depravity. The severed heads, a ghastly trophy collection, stood as a morbid testament to his inhumanity.

In an appalling crescendo of his violent spree, the killer's own mother became the final act of his gruesome symphony. In a twisted parody of retribution, he exacted his deep-seated vengeance, marking a perverse culmination of his murderous odyssey. The act was not just patricide but a symbol of his complete detachment from any semblance of humanity.

Kemper's eventual surrender to the authorities was as shocking as his crimes. His confession, detailed and unflinching, laid bare the extent of his brutality. Behind bars, the enormity of his actions etched into the annals of criminal history, the Co-Ed Butcher's story remains a chilling reminder of the profound darkness that can lurk within the human psyche.

The Surrender: Kemper's Own Endgame

In the annals of true crime, few stories are as chilling as that of Edmund Kemper, the Co-Ed Butcher. His towering figure, seemingly gentle demeanor, and intelligence formed a lethal combination that he used to terrifying effect. Prowling the roads of California, he preyed upon unsuspecting young women, their initial trust in this benign giant sealing their fates.

His modus operandi was as brutal as it was consistent. Luring his victims with a facade of safety, he quickly turned into a predator, exploiting their vulnerability. The horror that unfolded in the confines of his vehicle was both intimate and monstrous. His victims, overpowered and at his mercy, experienced a terror that was profound and personal.

The aftermath of each murder revealed the depth of Kemper's depravity. In the seclusion of his home, he transformed into a necromancer, performing unspeakable acts on the lifeless bodies. The dismemberment and defilement of his victims were rituals, reflecting a mind steeped in darkness and detachment from humanity.

The culmination of his ghastly spree was the murder of his own mother, a deed that epitomized his twisted psyche. This final act was not just a murder but a symbolic exorcism of his pent-up rage and hatred. The brutality he exhibited was a stark representation of his complex and disturbed relationship with her.

Kemper's eventual surrender to the authorities brought an end to his reign of terror but marked the beginning of a new chapter in criminal history. His confessions, clinical and devoid of remorse, painted a vivid picture of a man lost to his baser instincts. His story, a morbid tapestry woven from his gruesome acts, continues to haunt the field of criminal psychology and the public imagination alike.

Delving into Kemper's Psyche

Under the guise of a gentle giant, the Co-Ed Butcher, Edmund Kemper, wove a narrative of terror across California. His imposing stature and disarming persona were mere facades that concealed his true nature. With each unsuspecting young woman who entered his vehicle, a sinister plot unfolded. The serenity of their initial encounter, soon shattered by the realization of impending doom, marked the beginning of a nightmarish ordeal.

In the confines of his car, a macabre transformation occurred. The man who once seemed harmless morphed into a predator, his actions driven by a deep-seated malevolence. The screams and struggles of his victims were swallowed by the enclosing darkness, their fates sealed in moments of terror.

His home, a grotesque sanctuary for his morbid fascinations, bore witness to acts of unspeakable brutality. Here, Kemper indulged in his darkest impulses, the lifeless bodies of his victims desecrated in a chilling ritual. Each act of dismemberment was a testament to his detachment from empathy and humanity.

The zenith of his gruesome spree was marked by the murder of his own mother. This act, laden with symbolic significance, was a disturbing culmination of years of pent-up rage and resentment. In this singular act of patricide, Kemper's twisted psyche was laid bare, revealing a complex web of emotional turmoil and psychological dysfunction.

His eventual surrender to the authorities brought an end to a harrowing chapter in criminal history. The Co-Ed Butcher's confessions, devoid of remorse and filled with chilling detail, offered a glimpse into the mind of a man whose actions epitomized the extremities of human depravity. His legacy, a cautionary tale of the darkness that can lurk within, remains etched in the annals of true crime.

L: *Henry Lee Lucas*

From Drifter to Killer

In the desolate stillness of an abandoned building, the scene was anything but serene. Blood, like red paint flung in a fit of rage, splattered the crumbling walls and pooled into a macabre art on the cracked concrete floor. The air hung heavy, thick with the metallic stench of death. In the center, a figure lay sprawled, a grotesque marionette with strings cut. The killer had not been kind, carving into the victim's flesh with a precision that spoke of a morbid fascination with the human anatomy. Each incision was a testament to the perpetrator's chilling expertise and detachment, a silent scream etched into the lifeless form.

Lucas, in these moments of madness, became the artist of atrocity, his medium the very essence of life itself. His victims were more than just casualties; they were canvases upon which he expressed his darkest impulses. Their pleas and cries dissolved into the void, unheard and unheeded, as he meticulously dismantled their existence. Eyes, once bright with the spark of life, now stared emptily, bearing witness to the final terror they beheld. The surrounding chaos was a stark contrast to the killer's calm demeanor, a demeanor that belied the frenzied savagery of his actions.

As dawn broke, the light crept in, casting long shadows and illuminating the aftermath of the nocturnal nightmare. The once vibrant lives reduced to mere husks, discarded after the storm of violence had passed. The scene was a grim tapestry, woven with threads of pain and despair, a haunting reminder of the fragility of life. The authorities, upon discovering the scene, could scarcely comprehend the level of brutality, the inhumanity that one person could inflict upon another. The evidence was a twisted roadmap to a mind unhinged, a soul lost to the darkest corners of human potential.

The repercussions of these acts reverberated far beyond the crime scenes. Communities were gripped with fear, a palpable dread lingering in the air like a foul mist. Paranoia became the new norm, every stranger a potential monster lurking in plain sight. The killer's name was whispered in hushed tones, a boogeyman tale come to life, leaving an indelible mark on the psyche of a society grappling with the reality of pure evil among them. Each revelation, each gruesome detail that emerged, only served to deepen the collective trauma, a wound on the communal soul that would not easily heal.

In the end, the legacy left by this harbinger of death was one of pain, loss, and an unanswerable question: why? The search for understanding, for some semblance of reason in the senseless savagery, would prove as elusive as the shadows at twilight. The minds of those affected, forever haunted by the horrors witnessed, found little solace in the capture and conviction of the killer. For some evils, there are no words, no explanations that can mend the broken or bring back those who were taken. The story of Lucas and his reign of terror would forever be a chilling reminder of the darkness that can reside in the human heart.

The Confession Killer: True or False?

The moon hung low, casting an eerie pallor over the abandoned warehouse. Inside, the air was thick with the stench of decay, a pungent aroma that clawed at the senses. Shadows danced across the walls, the only witnesses to the carnage that lay within. There, sprawled across the cold, unforgiving concrete, was the latest offering to the killer's insatiable appetite for death. The body, a macabre masterpiece, was contorted in an unnatural pose, limbs twisted in silent agony. Deep, jagged cuts marred the flesh, each a testament to the killer's perverse desire to dominate and destroy.

He moved with a predator's grace, his actions not hurried but deliberate and precise. Each strike was a brushstroke on a canvas of skin and bone, his tools not of paint and palette but of steel and sinew. Blood, a crimson river, flowed freely, pooling around the lifeless form. It glistened in the dim light, a grotesque mirror reflecting the soul of the one who had taken so much more than just a life. The silence was oppressive, broken only by the soft drip of red, each drop a morbid metronome marking the passage of a life now extinguished.

The aftermath of his brutality was a tableau of horror, a grotesque still life that told a story of pain and terror. The air was heavy with the weight of unspeakable acts, the walls bearing silent testimony to the savagery inflicted within their confines. As the first rays of dawn began to pierce the darkness, they revealed the true extent of the desecration. It was a scene that would haunt the dreams of those who found it, a nightmarish vision that no amount of daylight could ever fully erase.

With each victim, the legend of the killer grew, a dark folklore woven from whispers and fear. The community lived in the shadow of this unseen menace, every creak and groan a potential herald of doom. Paranoia seeped into every home, a constant companion that whispered of danger lurking just out of sight. The police, desperate to end the reign of terror, found themselves always one step behind, their every effort seemingly anticipated and countered by a mind as cunning as it was cruel.

The story of this fiend was not just one of blood and death but of the darkest corners of the human psyche. It was a grim reminder of the monsters that walk among us, hidden behind the guise of the mundane. For those left in the wake of his destruction, the world would never be the same. The scars left behind were not just on the flesh of the victims but on the very soul of the community, a constant, aching reminder of the evil that had passed through their lives, leaving a trail of death and despair in its wake.

A Tangled Web of Lies and Murder

Beneath the cloak of night, a dilapidated house stood, its decrepit walls echoing the screams of the past. Inside, the air was saturated with the smell of rot and iron, a signature of the atrocities committed within. The floor was slick, a grotesque tapestry of blood and viscera, remnants of a life brutally taken. In the center, the latest victim lay, a twisted form of flesh and bone, their final expression one of abject terror. The killer had performed his grim ritual with a sadistic precision, each cut a deliberate desecration of the human form.

The perpetrator moved through the shadows, a specter of death, his mind a labyrinth of twisted fantasies. With each life taken, he plunged deeper into his own abyss, driven by a hunger that could never be sated. His hands, instruments of destruction, were coated in the lifeblood of his prey, a visceral testament to his dominion over life and death. The silence of the scene was a macabre symphony, the stillness punctuated only by the soft, sickening sounds of his work.

As dawn approached, the first light of day crept through the broken windows, casting long shadows over the scene of devastation. The once ordinary room was now an altar to his depravity, every surface telling a tale of pain and fear. The authorities, upon their grim discovery, were met with a vision of hell, a place where humanity was forsaken, and savagery reigned. The sheer brutality etched into every wound spoke of a mind unhinged, a being for whom life was nothing but a plaything to be broken and discarded.

Outside, the world remained oblivious to the nightmare within, the community unaware of the monster in their midst. Fear began to take root, spreading like a disease, its tendrils reaching into every home, every heart. The killer's name was whispered like a curse, a harbinger of death whose shadow fell over every quiet moment, turning peace into paranoia, tranquility into terror. The hunt for the fiend became a desperate race against time, a battle to protect the innocent from a fate too horrific to contemplate.

In the end, the saga of the killer was not just a tale of death, but a dark mirror reflecting the most depraved aspects of the human soul. It was a stark reminder of the thin veneer of civility that separates order from chaos, a warning of what lurks in the depths of the human heart. For those who gazed too long into the abyss, the memory of the horror would be etched into their very being, a scar that would never fade, a constant reminder of the darkness that had once walked among them, leaving a trail of blood and tears in its wake.

Media Frenzy and Public Outrage

The stench of decay permeated the air, a foul, clinging odor that announced the presence of death. In the dimly lit room, shadows clung to the corners, as if afraid to reveal the horror that lay within. A body, once a vessel of life, now lay desecrated, a grim showcase of the killer's handiwork. Deep, gaping wounds crisscrossed the flesh, each a silent testament to the savagery inflicted. The blood, now drying, painted a macabre picture, a final portrait of the victim's last agonizing moments.

Silently, the architect of this atrocity surveyed his work, his eyes reflecting not a glint of remorse but a perverse satisfaction. The scene before him was not one of tragedy but of triumph, a masterpiece wrought from human suffering. With each life he took, he felt not the weight of sin but the exhilaration of power, the divine thrill of holding dominion over life and death. The tools of his trade were simple yet effective, instruments that delivered pain and elicited fear with chilling efficiency.

As the night waned, the darkness outside began to retreat, but the darkness within the room—and within the killer's soul—remained, impenetrable and cold. The first light of dawn did little to dispel the sense of evil that clung to the place, an invisible shroud that muffled the sounds of the waking world outside. The killer knew his time was short; the daylight would bring discovery, and with it, the end of his macabre ritual. Yet, there was no hurry in his movements, only the methodical precision of one who knows his craft all too well.

In the streets beyond, life continued unabated, the city waking to another day, oblivious to the nightmare that had unfolded in its midst. The killer was but a phantom, a specter of death that vanished with the rising sun, leaving behind only the evidence of his existence. The community, once secure in the belief of their safety, now found themselves questioning every shadow, every stranger. Fear had taken root, spreading its tendrils through the heart of the city, a creeping dread that turned neighbor against neighbor, friend into potential foe.

The tale of this killer was a dark odyssey through the human psyche, a journey into the heart of darkness that resides within. It was a stark reminder of the thin line that separates man from monster, a line that, once crossed, can never be retraced. For those touched by the tragedy, life would never be the same; the scars left behind, both physical and emotional, would serve as a constant reminder of the evil that walked among them, a silent testament to the fragility of life and the proximity of death.

Lucas Under the Lens: A Clinical View

In the squalid darkness of an abandoned factory, the air was thick with the scent of blood and fear. The dim light barely revealed the figure sprawled on the ground, a grotesque tableau of human frailty. The victim's eyes, wide with the eternal shock of their final moments, stared into nothingness, their plea for mercy forever frozen in time. Around them, the evidence of the killer's fury was unmistakable; the deep, jagged lacerations spoke of a rage that was both wild and chillingly precise.

He stood over his work, a dark silhouette against the faint light, his breaths slow and measured amidst the chaos he had wrought. This was his domain, a realm where he was both judge and executioner, meting out his twisted version of justice with every strike. The silence was his alone to break, the stillness a canvas upon which he painted his nightmarish visions. His hands, stained with the lifeblood of another, were steady — the hands of a craftsman proud of his work.

As morning crept over the horizon, its light began to seep through the broken panes, casting long, accusing fingers across the scene. The killer's time was dwindling, the sanctuary of darkness retreating before the relentless advance of dawn. Yet, there was no haste in his departure, only the calm certainty of one who knows their craft intimately. He disappeared into the light, a specter of death melting away with the shadows, leaving behind a scene that would soon echo with the screams of the living.

Outside, the world stirred, unaware of the horror that had unfolded in its midst. The city, a living, breathing entity, continued its rhythmic pulse, each beat a reminder of the life that flowed through its streets. Yet, within its heart lay a darkness, a cancer that moved unseen, its appetite for destruction insatiable. The people, once secure in their routines, now glanced over their shoulders, their minds haunted by the knowledge that death had walked amongst them, its touch leaving an indelible stain upon their world.

The story of this phantom was a grim testament to the depths to which humanity could sink, a narrative woven from the pain and terror of its victims. It was a stark reminder that, beneath the veneer of civilization, lay a darkness waiting to be unleashed. For those who had looked into the abyss and seen the monster staring back, life would never regain its innocence; the shadows would always hold a hint of menace, and every stranger's face a potential mask hiding the inhuman gaze of a predator. The killer's legacy was one of blood and fear, a chapter of history written in the ink of human suffering.

M: *Herbert Mullin*

Mullin's Mind: The Early Signs

Herbert Mullin's descent into a morbid abyss began subtly, the first ripples appearing just after his high school triumphs. Beneath the veneer of a successful, promising youth lurked an insidious transformation, triggered by a personal tragedy. The loss of his close friend in a car accident, a seemingly random and brutal snatching of life, jolted his mental equilibrium. It was an invisible fracture, widening slowly, unnoticed by those around him.

In the solitude of his emerging adulthood, Mullin encountered the beguiling allure of psychedelic substances. Cannabis and LSD became his frequent companions, catalyzing a slide into a warped reality. These substances didn't just alter his mind; they amplified the brewing chaos within. By 21, his family started to see the disturbing signs: erratic behavior, disjointed thoughts, a young man drifting further from reality.

Amidst the tumult of his inner world, Mullin sought refuge in hospitals and therapy sessions, yet he remained a prisoner to his escalating delusions. His mental landscape, once fertile with potential, became a breeding ground for paranoia and darkness. The voices began as whispers, morphing into commanding presences that echoed his deepest fears and desires. By 23, he was a mosaic of fractured thoughts, diagnosed schizophrenically by multiple doctors, yet the true depth of his turmoil remained hidden, festering.

As Mullin's reality crumbled, he latched onto a bizarre and macabre belief: the prevention of catastrophic earthquakes through human sacrifice. This conviction wasn't a sudden revelation but a delusion that had been gestating for years. Letters to the UN, disjointed notes, and a fixation on the date of his birth linked to the 1906 San Francisco earthquake all pointed to a mind caught in a labyrinth of its own making. His reasoning was twisted, a grotesque tapestry woven from threads of insanity and obsession.

Mullin's gruesome odyssey into murder began on a fateful day in October 1972. He chose a transient man as his first victim, believing him to be a biblical figure who had telepathically sought death at Mullin's hands. The act was savage, an unleashing of pent-up madness. It marked the beginning of a series of killings, each more brutal than the last, driven by the chilling belief that each life taken was a step towards averting a natural calamity. His victims, selected with a terrifying randomness, became unwilling participants in his deranged crusade against imagined disasters.

Ritual and Reason: The Santa Cruz Murders

In the early 1970s, the serene landscape of Santa Cruz was shattered by a series of chilling murders. These were not mere acts of violence, but ritualistic killings, steeped in a macabre logic understood only by their perpetrator. The first victim, Lawrence White, was bludgeoned to death with a bat, his body left as an eerie testament to the killer's emerging pattern.

Each murder was more gruesome than the last. Mary Guilfoyle's life was brutally cut short; her body dismembered and discarded like refuse along a desolate road. The killer's descent into madness was marked by an increasing disregard for human life, a terrifying devaluation that culminated in a most shocking act: the murder of Father Henri Tomei. The priest was savagely stabbed in his own confessional, a sacred space defiled by an act of incomprehensible violence.

The killer's rationale, fueled by delusions of grandeur and a twisted sense of duty, drove him to seek out more victims. A young couple, an innocent family, and a group of teenagers camping peacefully – all were ensnared in his deadly web. Each murder was executed with a cold, calculated precision, devoid of any semblance of humanity.

As the body count rose, so did the killer's conviction in his misguided mission. He believed he was the sole barrier between the world and an apocalyptic earthquake. This belief propelled him further into the abyss of his own insanity, each murder an attempt to stave off a disaster only he could foresee.

The final act of violence, the murder of a man in broad daylight, was the culmination of a reign of terror that had gripped Santa Cruz. The killer's capture marked the end of a nightmare, but the scars left by his actions would forever haunt the community. His twisted logic, born from a mind unraveled by mental illness and delusion, had wrought destruction that would echo through the annals of criminal history.

Voices to Violence: Mullin's Motivations Detail

The twisted mind of Mullin was a cauldron of delusional thoughts, simmering with a bizarre blend of religious fervor and apocalyptic fear. He believed that his killings were not mere acts of violence but a sacred duty to prevent a catastrophic earthquake. This conviction stemmed from a deep-seated belief in the supernatural power of human sacrifice, a principle he thought was embedded in the very fabric of the universe.

As Mullin navigated through his distorted reality, the voices in his head became his unwavering guides. They whispered macabre instructions, convincing him of his unique role as a savior against natural disasters. These auditory hallucinations weren't fleeting; they were constant companions, reinforcing his gruesome mission with each passing day.

His targets were chosen not for personal vendettas but as symbols in his grand, twisted narrative. Each victim was a sacrificial offering to the gods of his deranged cosmos, a necessary act to maintain the delicate balance of life and death. The randomness of his selection process only heightened the terror he inflicted upon the community, as no one was safe from being chosen as his next offering.

As he carried out his killings, Mullin's methods were marked by a chilling efficiency. He moved with the precision of a man convinced of his divine purpose, each murder an essential step in his quest to avert a seismic apocalypse. This methodical approach to killing revealed a deeply entrenched belief in the righteousness of his actions.

Mullin's journey from a troubled youth to a serial killer was a testament to the catastrophic consequences of untreated mental illness. His descent into violence was not just a personal tragedy but a harrowing reminder of the thin line between sanity and madness. His story is a chilling narrative of how the human mind, once lost in the shadows of delusion, can become capable of unspeakable horrors.

The Arrest: Ending the Killings

The downfall of Mullin was as abrupt as it was dramatic. His final act of violence, a brazen daylight shooting, left a community in shock and set the wheels of justice in motion. A vigilant neighbor, noting the killer's license plate, became the unexpected hero in this dark saga. The police swiftly traced the number, closing in on the man who had cast a shadow of terror over Santa Cruz.

His capture was devoid of the dramatic confrontations often seen in such cases. Mullin offered no resistance, almost as if he had resigned himself to his fate. The tranquility of his surrender belied the brutality of his crimes, a chilling contrast that left the arresting officers unnerved.

In the interrogation room, the horror of his actions began to unfurl. Mullin, with unsettling calmness, recounted the details of his gruesome campaign. Each confession peeled back layers of his twisted psyche, revealing a man lost in a delusional labyrinth of his own making. His words painted a vivid picture of the chaos he had unleashed, a narrative punctuated by his belief in the necessity of his actions.

As the trial loomed, the community grappled with the magnitude of his crimes. The courtroom became the stage where the final act of Mullin's tragic story would play out. Prosecutors meticulously built a case, weaving together the gruesome details of each murder, while the defense delved into the murky depths of his troubled mind.

The conviction of Mullin brought a semblance of closure to a community ravaged by fear. Yet, the scars he left behind were indelible, a haunting reminder of the fragility of the human psyche and the devastating impact of unchecked mental illness. His story, a grim tapestry of violence and madness, remains etched in the annals of criminal history, a sobering testament to the darkest corners of the human mind.

Mullin's Madness: Clinical Examination

The clinical dissection of Mullin's psyche offered a grim window into the mind of a serial killer. Psychiatric evaluations painted a picture of a deeply disturbed individual, tormented by hallucinations and delusions. His belief in the necessity of murder to prevent natural disasters was not a sudden break from reality, but the culmination of years of mental deterioration.

Experts delved into his past, uncovering a history of drug use that likely exacerbated his latent schizophrenia. It was a potent mix of psychotropic substances and mental illness that created a perfect storm, propelling him towards violence. His descent into madness was gradual, marked by increasing paranoia and a disconnection from reality.

In his own twisted logic, Mullin saw himself as a savior, chosen to protect the world from catastrophic earthquakes. This belief was not mere fancy but a conviction as real to him as any physical law. His birthday, coinciding with the date of the 1906 San Francisco earthquake, only reinforced his delusional sense of destiny.

The psychiatrists also unraveled his complex relationship with sexuality and religion, elements that featured prominently in his distorted worldview. Mullin's writings revealed a mind grappling with themes of sin, sacrifice, and redemption, all interwoven into his justification for murder.

Ultimately, the clinical examination of Mullin did more than just outline the contours of his madness. It shed light on the tragic consequences of untreated mental illness and the importance of early intervention. His case remains a cautionary tale, a stark reminder of the depths to which the human mind can sink when lost in the shadowy realms of psychosis.

N: *Earle Nelson*

Nelson's Nefarious Beginnings

In the shadowy corners of San Francisco's residential streets, a silent predator lurked, his presence marked by a chilling calmness that belied the monstrous intent within. The Gorilla Man, as he would later be known, moved with a deceptive gentleness, a facade meticulously crafted to disarm. His victims, often unsuspecting middle-aged landladies, were lured by his facade of piety and need for shelter. But behind the mask of the meek drifter was a heart devoid of mercy, pulsing with a dark, insatiable hunger.

His method was as methodical as it was macabre. He would carefully select his prey, often through innocuous 'room for rent' ads, and upon entering their homes under the guise of a potential tenant, he would unleash his true, sinister nature. The Gorilla Man's hands, large and powerful, were instruments of death, wrapping around the throats of his victims in a vice-like grip. The life of each woman was extinguished in a brutal, intimate act of strangulation, their final moments a harrowing struggle against a force too overpowering to overcome.

But the horror did not cease with the cessation of breath. In the eerie silence that followed, he committed acts of necrophilia, a grotesque violation that further desecrated the sanctity of the dead. Each crime scene was a tableau of terror, the twisted culmination of a deranged mind's desires. The victims, once vibrant beings, were reduced to mere objects in his macabre ritual, their humanity stripped away in the most vile manner imaginable.

The Gorilla Man's reign of terror left a bloody trail across the West Coast, each murder a grotesque echo of the last. The communities, once havens of tranquility, were now gripped by fear, their peace shattered by the knowledge of the beast that walked among them. The police, desperate to end the carnage, found themselves grappling with a cunning adversary, always one step ahead, his identity shrouded in mystery.

In the end, it was his own hubris that led to his downfall. The Gorilla Man's overconfidence betrayed him, and he was ensnared by the very law enforcement he had so skillfully evaded. His capture brought a collective sigh of relief, yet the scars he left on the psyche of a nation were indelible. He had become a dark symbol of the evil that can hide behind the most unassuming façade, a reminder of the depths of depravity to which humanity can sink.

The Gorilla Man: A Cross-Country Terror

The moonlit streets of Portland whispered secrets of a lurking terror, an unseen menace that hunted in the shadows. This predator, a figure of nightmarish proportions, moved with a sinister grace, his intentions as dark as the alleys he frequented. He preyed upon the unsuspecting, his eyes scanning for his next victim, an innocent life to be snuffed out in a twisted ritual of violence and death.

His approach was deceptively charming, a wolf cloaked in sheep's clothing. He slithered into the lives of his targets, often vulnerable women seeking tenants for their boarding rooms. These women, unaware of the danger, welcomed him with open arms, oblivious to the fact that they were inviting death into their homes. His smile, warm and reassuring, was a mask that concealed the cold, sadistic heart beating within.

As night fell, the true horror began. His hands, instruments of cruelty, wrapped around the throats of his victims, squeezing the life out of them in a slow, agonizing dance of death. The struggle, a desperate fight for survival, was futile against his overpowering strength. The lifeless bodies, left behind like discarded puppets, bore the gruesome signature of his heinous acts.

But the nightmare did not end with the act of killing. In the stillness that followed, he committed unspeakable acts upon the corpses, his twisted desires defiling the sanctity of death. Each crime scene was a macabre display of his dark fantasies, a chilling testament to the depths of his depravity. The aftermath of his brutality left communities in a state of shock and despair, the memory of his atrocities forever etched in their collective consciousness.

The hunt for this phantom of death was relentless, a race against time to stop the carnage. The police, determined to bring an end to his reign of terror, pieced together the clues, their resolve unyielding. Yet, he remained elusive, a ghost in the night, always one step ahead. His capture, when it finally came, was a moment of triumph mixed with horror, the end of a nightmare that had held a city in its grip. His legacy, however, was a somber reminder of the evil that can lurk within the human soul, a chilling portrait of the monster that can hide beneath a façade of normalcy.

Chasing a Shadow: The Hunt for Nelson

Under the guise of night, he prowled, a specter haunting the quiet streets. His presence was a dark omen, foreboding a terror that would soon grip the hearts of a community. With each step, he neared his unsuspecting prey, women who believed they were safe within the confines of their own homes. His eyes gleamed with a malevolent intent, a stark contrast to the reassuring smile he offered to those he was about to destroy.

The encounters began innocuously, a simple knock on the door, a polite inquiry about a room for rent. His victims, lulled into a false sense of security by his seemingly benign demeanor, failed to see the monster lurking beneath. Once inside, the facade fell away, revealing the true horror of his intentions. Their homes, once sanctuaries, became their final battlegrounds.

His attacks were brutal, a savage unleashing of pent-up fury. His victims' final moments were filled with unimaginable terror as they struggled against his overpowering strength. He strangled them, his hands tightening around their necks with a merciless grip, extinguishing their lives in a prolonged moment of agony. The intimacy of the act, the feeling of life slipping away under his fingers, was his perverse gratification.

In the aftermath, the silence of the crime scenes was deafening. The lifeless bodies of his victims lay in a macabre tableau, a testament to the night's atrocities. He defiled them further in death, a final act of domination and desecration. Each crime scene was a chilling masterpiece of his dark desires, a grotesque display of his control over life and death.

As the killings continued, a palpable fear settled over the city. The hunt for the murderer became a desperate race against time. Detectives scoured for clues, piecing together the fragmented puzzle of his identity. The community held its breath, waiting for the nightmare to end. When his reign of terror was finally brought to a close, relief washed over the city. Yet, the scars left behind were indelible, a haunting reminder of the evil that had walked among them, hidden in plain sight.

Nelson's Capture and Trial

In the dead of night, an ominous figure roamed, his silhouette barely distinguishable in the dimly lit streets. He was an architect of terror, crafting his sinister legacy with each unsuspecting victim. The quiet neighborhoods, once symbols of suburban tranquility, unwittingly played host to his macabre performances. Behind each curtained window lay a potential stage for his next act of horror.

He approached his victims under the guise of innocence, his demeanor disarmingly calm. Women, alone and unsuspecting, were his preferred targets. Their homes, which should have been safe havens, transformed into theaters of brutality. The killer's method was unhurried, calculated, revealing a chilling patience. He relished the power he wielded at that moment, the power to inflict fear and pain.

His method of murder was as personal as it was gruesome. Strangulation, a direct and intimate means, allowed him to watch the life drain from his victims' eyes. There was no quick release for them; their last moments were prolonged, agonizing, filled with a terror that only he could inflict. The intimacy of the act seemed to fuel his twisted desires, each death a perverse artwork of his own creation.

After the life had been cruelly wrung from their bodies, he would continue his desecration. His acts of necrophilia, heinous violations of the dead, added a further layer of horror to his crimes. The scenes he left behind were stomach-churning, the air heavy with the stench of death and the palpable echo of unspeakable acts. These crime scenes were not just evidence of murder but of a deep, unrelenting evil.

As the body count rose, so did the fear in the community. The police, grappling with the weight of the killer's elusive presence, worked tirelessly. The urgency was palpable - each moment that passed could mean another life lost. When the killer was finally apprehended, the relief was overshadowed by the weight of his atrocities. His capture ended a chapter of terror, but the scars he left on the psyche of the community would never fully heal.

Inside Nelson's Mind: A Clinical Perspective

The city's heartbeat slowed under the cloak of night, but for him, this was the time to come alive. His shadow slithered through the alleyways, a harbinger of the unspeakable horrors that were to unfold. In his mind, a symphony of screams played, orchestrating his next move. The unsuspecting city, its residents nestled in their beds, was unaware that they harbored a beast in their midst, one who reveled in the macabre.

His victims, chosen not for who they were but for what they represented, were mere pawns in his twisted game. Women, he believed, were the perfect embodiment of vulnerability and thus, the ideal subjects for his cruel experiments. He would watch them, learn their routines, and strike when they least expected it. The element of surprise was not just a tactic; it was part of the thrill.

The manner of their deaths was a ritual in itself. He didn't just kill; he annihilated their very essence. Strangulation was his chosen method, a way to feel the life ebb away from their bodies under the pressure of his grip. It was intimate, personal, and for him, deeply satisfying. The act of taking life was not enough; he had to feel it leaving their bodies, a power he deemed his and his alone.

In the aftermath, he would sit with his lifeless victims, admiring his handiwork. To him, their bodies were not vessels of life but canvases on which he painted his story of control and dominance. The scenes he left behind were a chaotic blend of blood and terror, each telling the tale of a struggle that ended in the most gruesome manner.

When he finally vanished into the shadows from whence he came, he left behind a trail of destruction, a community shaken to its core. The police were always a step behind, grappling with the brutal reality of a predator in their midst. Each crime scene was a stark reminder of the fragility of life and the depths of depravity one man could sink. His capture brought an end to the carnage but the scars he left, both physical and psychological, would forever linger in the annals of the city's history.

O: *The Ominous Outsiders*

The Fringe Figures: Serial Killers Outside the Norm

Serial killers who deviate from the typical profiles challenge our understanding of criminal psychology. They're the enigmatic figures who don't fit neatly into boxes, often defying the categorizations established by criminologists and psychologists alike. One such individual is Richard Chase, known as "The Vampire of Sacramento," whose gruesome acts in the late 1970s were driven by delusions and a profound disconnection from reality. Chase's actions were not the calculated moves of a cold-blooded killer but the erratic spasms of a deeply disturbed mind, illustrating the complex interplay between severe mental illness and homicidal behavior.

Equally perplexing are the cases of killers driven by unusual motives, far removed from the more 'common' drivers like greed, revenge, or sexual sadism. Consider Leonarda Cianciulli, the Italian serial killer who believed she could protect her son's life in World War II through human sacrifice, turning her victims into soap and teacakes. Her story is not just one of murder but of folklore and superstition twisted into a macabre reality.

These outliers challenge the stereotypes of serial killers as either cold, calculating predators or charismatic manipulators. Their stories shed light on the less traversed paths of human psychology, where deep-seated issues manifest in tragically violent ways. As society seeks to understand and prevent such heinous acts, studying these fringe figures offers invaluable insights into the darkest corners of the human psyche.

The Outcasts: Examining Social Pariahs Turned Killers

In the grim tableau of serial killers, certain individuals stand out not just for their crimes but for their profound alienation from society. These are the outcasts, whose journeys into darkness are often marked by a life spent on the fringes, where the cold winds of isolation gnaw at the edges of their psyche. A vivid illustration of this is the tale of Ed Gein, the infamous inspiration behind cinematic horror icons. Gein's existence was one of utter seclusion, crafting a macabre world from the remains of his victims, a world where human skins became garments and skulls turned into bowls. His home in Plainfield, Wisconsin, became a grotesque museum of his alienation and derangement.

Across the ocean, in the rugged landscapes of Russia, Andrei Chikatilo, known as the Rostov Ripper, lived a life marred by chronic social awkwardness and rejection. His inability to forge meaningful connections led him down a path of horrific violence, claiming the lives of over 50 victims. Chikatilo's story is a chilling testament to the destructive potential of a life lived in the shadows of society.

These individuals, with their histories of social exile and emotional detachment, provide a stark canvas upon which the devastating impact of isolation is painted in vivid, blood-red strokes. Their descent into murder is a journey through a desolate landscape of the human condition, where the absence of connection and empathy breeds monsters in the shape of men. As we delve into the lives of these outcasts, we're forced to confront the unsettling truth that within the deep chasms of isolation, something profoundly disturbing can take root and flourish.

The Lone Wolves: Isolation and Its Impact on Serial Killers

Isolation is a silent predator, its impact often unnoticed until it has hollowed out its victim, leaving behind a shell where empathy and humanity once resided. This is the story of the lone wolves, the serial killers whose isolation was both a catalyst for and a consequence of their heinous acts. Take, for example, the case of Ted Kaczynski, also known as the Unabomber. His retreat into the seclusion of a Montana cabin was not just a physical withdrawal from society but a descent into a maelstrom of anger and paranoia. His isolation became the incubator for his deadly campaign, reflecting a mind untethered from the moderating influence of social interaction.

Then there's Dennis Rader, the BTK Killer, who, despite maintaining a facade of normalcy, harbored a deep-seated alienation from those around him. His double life epitomizes the hidden chasm between the public self and the private, isolated self, where monstrous thoughts fester and grow. Rader's story is a chilling reminder that isolation can exist in plain sight, its corrosive effects hidden behind the mundane mask of everyday life.

These lone wolves roam the bleak landscape of their own psyche, disconnected from the warmth of human connection. Their paths are marked by the devastating impact of their solitude, a force that shapes their twisted perceptions and fuels their dark urges. As society seeks to understand and curb the tide of serial violence, the stories of these isolated killers stand as stark reminders of the profound and often destructive power of isolation.

Obscure Motives: Understanding the Less Common Killers

In the shadowy realm of serial murder, where motivations are often as murky as the deeds themselves, there exists a subset of killers driven by obscure, often unfathomable reasons. Their motives are cryptic enigmas, challenging the very limits of our understanding. Delve into the mind of Joseph James DeAngelo, the Golden State Killer, whose reign of terror across California was not solely about violence but a complex web of psychological compulsion, power, and control. His actions were a dark dance of dominance, a twisted performance on the stage of his victims' lives.

Then, consider the puzzling case of Dorothea Puente, the seemingly benign elderly woman who transformed her boarding house into a tomb for her vulnerable tenants. Her motives were entangled in a web of greed and a perverse desire for control, her nurturing facade masking a heart as cold as the graves in her garden.

These killers defy simple categorization, their motives a labyrinth of dark desires and twisted logic. They are the human embodiment of the inexplicable, a stark reminder of the unfathomable depths of human depravity. As we seek to understand them, we find ourselves peering into an abyss, where the lines between sanity and madness blur, and where the most chilling aspect is not just the act of killing, but the incomprehensible reasons behind it.

Outsider Minds: Psychological Analysis of Atypical Killers

In the clinical dissection of the minds of atypical serial killers, psychologists and criminologists strive to unravel the complex web of factors that contribute to their deviant behavior. These individuals often exhibit psychological profiles that deviate significantly from the norm, challenging existing theories and models of criminal psychology. Consider the case of Aileen Wuornos, a female serial killer whose history of abuse and marginalization provides a stark contrast to the more common male-dominated narratives. Wuornos's life and crimes highlight the interplay between psychological trauma, societal alienation, and violent retribution.

Similarly, the peculiar case of Herbert Mullin, who believed his killings could prevent earthquakes, offers a window into the world of psychosis and its role in driving homicidal behavior. Mullin's delusions and disorganized thinking are symptomatic of a deeply disturbed mind, one that operates on a logic entirely its own.

Through a clinical lens, these outlier killers represent a challenge to conventional understanding. Their cases force a reevaluation of the psychological models used to understand serial killers, pushing experts to consider a broader spectrum of mental health issues, personality disorders, and environmental factors. In studying these atypical minds, the field of forensic psychology not only gains a deeper understanding of the extremes of human behavior but also enhances its ability to potentially predict and prevent future tragedies.

P: *Christopher Peterson*

The Southside Slayer: An Unseen Force

In the chill of an October night in 1990, Indiana streets became a hunting ground. A figure, shrouded in darkness, prowled the quiet neighborhoods, a shotgun his chilling companion. The first blast shattered the silence, its echoing roar a death knell. Blood splattered on the concrete, a macabre painting under the dim streetlights. The victim lay motionless, their life extinguished in a brutal instant.

The following weeks saw a crescendo of terror. Each nightfall brought with it a palpable dread, an anticipation of horror. Doors were bolted, windows sealed, but the fear permeated every household. The killer moved like a specter, unseen yet omnipresent. His weapon roared, and lives were snuffed out, one after another. The streets that once echoed with the sounds of life now resonated with the echoes of shotgun blasts and the cries of the dying.

Peterson, the orchestrator of this nightmare, was a master of evasion. His movements were unpredictable, his choices of victims random. There was no pattern, no predictability, nothing that could give the authorities a clue. Blood-stained sidewalks and the haunting sound of sirens became the night's new normal. The city was held hostage by fear, every resident a potential target in this deadly game.

The investigation became a desperate race against time. Each new crime scene was a grotesque tableau, a visceral display of Peterson's ruthlessness. Forensic teams worked tirelessly, searching for the elusive clue that would lead to the predator's capture. Meanwhile, the body count rose, each victim a tragic testament to the killer's cold-blooded efficiency.

The eventual arrest of Peterson didn't bring immediate relief. The trials that followed were a labyrinth of legal complexities, each turn revealing more about the enigmatic and merciless mind of the Southside Slayer. The courtrooms were packed, the air thick with anticipation and the heavy burden of justice. Each revelation, each piece of evidence, peeled back layers of the horror that had gripped Indiana, leaving a scar that would long outlast the trials.

Terror in the Streets: The Chicago Murders

The Chicago streets, once bustling with life, transformed into a canvas of horror as Peterson's spree unfolded. Echoes of shotgun blasts pierced the night, each a grim punctuation to the city's newfound nightmare. Bloodstained pavements and shattered glass bore silent witness to the carnage. Victims, caught in the wrong place at the wrong time, met their end in a spray of buckshot, their final moments a symphony of fear and confusion.

Under the cold gaze of streetlights, his silhouette loomed, a harbinger of death. With each pull of the trigger, he carved his name into the annals of infamy. The randomness of his attacks left the city in a grip of paranoia. No one knew where the killer would strike next, the unpredictability amplifying the terror. He moved through the shadows, a ghost leaving nothing but destruction in his wake.

In these darkened alleys and deserted corners, the predator found his stage. The screams of his victims were muffled by the urban cacophony, their pleas for mercy lost in the void. His cold, unfeeling eyes mirrored the brutality of his actions, a man devoid of empathy, driven by an insatiable urge to kill.

The aftermath of each attack was a grotesque scene, a tableau of horror and despair. The air was heavy with the metallic tang of blood and the acrid smell of gunpowder. Police sirens wailed in the distance, a futile lament for lives brutally cut short. Forensic teams scoured the scenes, collecting the remnants of the killer's rage, hoping to piece together the puzzle of his madness.

As the body count rose, the city held its breath, each day dawning with the dread of another attack. The killer, now a specter haunting Chicago, became the subject of whispered conversations and frantic media speculation. The fear he instilled was palpable, a dark cloud hanging over the city, its residents waiting with bated breath for the end of this macabre dance with death.

Peterson's Prowess: Evading Capture

Night after night, the city's heartbeats synced with the ominous rhythm of a shotgun's blasts. Peterson, the shadowy figure orchestrating this terror, moved with chilling precision. His ability to vanish into the urban labyrinth after each attack was uncanny. The streets, a maze of potential hideouts, served as his sanctuary, a dark embrace that shielded him from the grasp of justice.

As the city lay ensnared in his web of fear, law enforcement agencies cast a wide net, desperate to catch the elusive phantom. They combed through neighborhoods, dissected every lead, every whisper of his existence. Yet, he remained a ghost, a whisper of dread on the wind. His ability to remain unseen, undetected, was a testament to his dark artistry, a morbid game of cat and mouse played on a city-wide scale.

The investigations, rife with urgency, turned over every stone, every shadowed corner, seeking a clue, a trace of his passage. But Peterson was always one step ahead, a master of evasion. His knowledge of the city's underbelly, its forgotten passages and hidden enclaves, rendered him virtually invisible. Each new sunrise brought with it not relief, but a grim acknowledgment of his continued freedom.

In this grim narrative, the hunter and the hunted engaged in a relentless dance. The police, bound by duty and driven by the cries of the victims' families, pushed forward. Peterson, fueled by a dark compulsion, reveled in the chase, the fear he sowed, the power he wielded. It was a twisted game, played on the edge of morality, each party driven by their own set of rules.

The city, held in the grip of this macabre drama, watched with bated breath. The saga of the hunter and the hunted, of predator and prey, was etched into its history. Peterson's evasion of capture became the stuff of legend, a dark tale whispered in the corridors of law enforcement and amongst the frightened citizens, a chilling reminder of the thin veil between safety and chaos.

The Trial: Justice for the Victims

In the sterile confines of the courtroom, a different kind of terror unfolded. Here, the gruesome details of Peterson's reign of horror were laid bare, each testimony a stark window into the depths of his brutality. The air was thick with tension, the collective breath of the audience held in suspense as witnesses recounted the chilling tales. Each word, each description, painted a vivid, blood-soaked picture of the nights that had paralyzed a city.

Prosecutors, armed with a mountain of evidence and fueled by a fervent desire for justice, wove a narrative of the killer's cold and methodical approach. They displayed crime scene photos, a visual cacophony of gore and violence, each image searing into the minds of the jurors. The stark reality of his actions, unfiltered and graphic, filled the courtroom, an oppressive reminder of the lives brutally extinguished.

In stark contrast, the defense's efforts to humanize Peterson seemed almost surreal amid the litany of his crimes. They painted a picture of a troubled man, a narrative met with skepticism and disdain. The courtroom became an arena, a battleground of facts and emotions, where the scales of justice wavered precariously between punishment and understanding.

As the trial progressed, the families of the victims sat in silent vigil, their faces etched with grief and longing. Their eyes, hollow with loss, followed every word, every piece of evidence. For them, the trial was more than a quest for justice; it was a search for closure, a desperate grasp at understanding the senseless cruelty that had befallen their loved ones.

When the verdict was finally delivered, a palpable wave of relief mixed with sorrow swept through the courtroom. Peterson, now condemned by his own actions and the weight of evidence against him, faced the consequences of his heinous spree. The trial, a harrowing journey through the darkest alleys of human nature, closed a chapter on a saga of fear, but it left behind scars that would endure, a haunting legacy of the terror that had gripped the heart of the city.

Peterson's Psychological Profile

Delving into the psyche of Peterson was akin to navigating a labyrinth of shadows and despair. Experts probed the depths of his mind, seeking to unravel the tangled threads of thought and emotion that drove him to such heinous acts. His blank expressions in court, a stark contrast to the ferocity of his crimes, suggested a complex and disturbed inner world, a mind haunted by demons only he could see.

Forensic psychologists speculated on the catalysts of his rage. Was it a childhood marred by trauma, a series of events that warped his perception of right and wrong? Or was it a deeper, more intrinsic flaw in his psychological makeup? These questions hung in the air, unanswered but heavy with implication. The courtroom became a theater where theories of mental instability, personality disorders, and the nature of evil were all dissected under the unforgiving light of scrutiny.

Witnesses to his demeanor described him as an enigma, a man of contradictions. To some, he appeared almost normal, capable of mundane interactions, masking the turmoil that roiled beneath. To others, he was a figure of intimidation, his presence alone enough to evoke an instinctual sense of unease. This duality perplexed even the most seasoned experts, a puzzle of human behavior that defied easy categorization.

The exploration of his psyche was not just a clinical exercise; it was a journey into the heart of darkness. Each revelation, each hypothesis, shed light on the fractured nature of a murderer's mind. Yet, with each step closer to understanding, the sheer magnitude of his detachment from humanity became more apparent, a chasm too vast and shadowed to fully comprehend.

The legacy of Peterson's psyche was a tapestry of horror and fascination, a reminder of the unfathomable depths to which the human mind can descend. His profile stood as a grim testament to the complexities of the criminal mind, a subject of study that would continue to challenge and disturb long after his name faded from the headlines.

Q: *Questions and Quandaries*

The Evolution of Criminal Profiling

The origins of criminal profiling trace back to the late 19th century, marking a significant shift in criminology and forensic science. This evolution was not an overnight transformation but a gradual accumulation of methodologies and insights.

One pivotal moment occurred in 1888, with the infamous Jack the Ripper case in London. Police surgeons George Phillips and Thomas Bond attempted to infer the characteristics of the perpetrator based on the gruesome nature of the crimes. Though rudimentary by today's standards, their efforts laid the groundwork for what would eventually become criminal profiling.

Fast forward to the 1940s, a notable advancement came from Dr. Walter C. Langer, a Harvard psychologist. Commissioned by the Office of Strategic Services (OSS), the precursor to the CIA, Langer produced a groundbreaking psychological profile of Adolf Hitler. His analysis, though speculative in parts, accurately predicted several aspects of Hitler's behavior, further legitimizing the practice of profiling.

The 1950s and 1960s saw the FBI gradually adopt and refine techniques of criminal profiling. Pioneers like Howard Teten and Patrick Mullany began applying psychological principles to criminal investigations, a practice that became more structured under the influence of FBI agents like John E. Douglas and Robert Ressler in the 1970s. Their work, including the introduction of the term 'serial killer,' revolutionized the field, introducing concepts like crime scene analysis and the classification of murderers into organized and disorganized categories.

This era also witnessed the integration of profiling into mainstream law enforcement. Profilers began collaborating with detectives, offering insights into the minds of unknown perpetrators, which proved crucial in numerous investigations. The development of profiling software and databases in the late 20th century further enhanced the efficiency and accuracy of criminal profiling.

Today, criminal profiling is an amalgamation of psychology, forensics, and detective work. It continues to evolve with advancements in technology and psychology, striving for greater accuracy in understanding the most complex criminal minds.

Profiling Breakthroughs: Case Studies

The canvas of criminal profiling is richly painted with instances of breakthroughs, each a testament to the evolving science and art of understanding the criminal mind. These case studies shine a light on the intricate dance between profiler and perpetrator, where each clue serves as a brushstroke in the larger portrait of the criminal.

Consider the case of the Green River Killer, Gary Ridgway, who evaded capture for nearly two decades. It was the meticulous profiling by Robert Keppel and John E. Douglas that eventually led to his capture in 2001. Their profile, detailed and vividly accurate, described not just the psychological traits of Ridgway but also his likely physical characteristics and habits. The eventual arrest of Ridgway was a landmark moment, demonstrating the power of well-crafted profiling in apprehending elusive serial killers.

Another notable instance is the Mad Bomber of New York City, George Metesky, active in the 1940s and 1950s. Criminal profiler James Brussel's near-clairvoyant profile of Metesky is legendary. Brussel predicted the bomber's age, marital status, ethnicity, and even his attire. When Metesky was finally apprehended, he matched the profile with eerie precision. This case not only underscored the efficacy of profiling but also helped gain public and law enforcement trust in the method.

The BTK (Bind, Torture, Kill) killer, Dennis Rader, presents another remarkable study. Rader, who terrorized Wichita, Kansas, over several decades, was eventually caught through a combination of traditional police work and profiling insights that provided a psychological blueprint of the killer. The profile helped narrow down the suspect pool, leading to Rader's capture in 2005.

These cases, among others, serve as landmarks in the journey of criminal profiling. They exemplify the blend of intuition, psychological acumen, and investigative rigor that marks the discipline. Each solved case not only brought justice but also added a new layer of depth and sophistication to the science of profiling, making it an indispensable tool in the arsenal against serial killers.

Controversies in Profiling Techniques

The field of criminal profiling, while groundbreaking, is not without its controversies. These debates center around the validity, accuracy, and application of profiling techniques in the pursuit of serial killers.

One major contention lies in the reliance on psychological assumptions. Critics argue that profiling often leans heavily on stereotypical assumptions about mental health and behavior. For instance, the assumption that certain behavioral patterns or childhood traumas are indicative of a propensity for serial killing can be overly simplistic and sometimes misleading. This critique raises questions about the ethical implications of such generalizations and their impact on investigations.

Another controversy involves the accuracy and predictive power of profiles. High-profile errors in profiling have occasionally led to wrongful accusations or the pursuit of incorrect leads. The case of the Atlanta Child Murders in the early 1980s serves as a notable example. The initial profile of the perpetrator significantly differed from the actual killer, Wayne Williams, leading to a delay in his apprehension. Such instances underscore the fallibility of profiling and the need for constant refinement.

Additionally, the debate extends to the scientific basis of profiling. Some scholars argue that profiling is more art than science, lacking the empirical rigor typically associated with scientific methods. The subjective nature of profile creation, often based on the profiler's intuition and experience, can vary significantly between profilers, leading to inconsistencies in the quality and accuracy of profiles.

Despite these controversies, it is important to recognize that criminal profiling has evolved over the years, incorporating more scientific methods and data analysis. Advances in psychology, forensics, and technology are continually shaping and refining profiling techniques, aiming to address these criticisms.

The ongoing debate in criminal profiling reflects the complex nature of understanding and predicting human behavior, especially in the context of extreme criminality. While it remains a valuable tool in criminal investigations, its limitations and the controversies surrounding it serve as a reminder of the need for continuous scrutiny and improvement in the field.

Profiling's Impact on Investigations

The integration of criminal profiling into law enforcement investigations has been akin to a dramatic orchestration, with each case unfolding like a complex symphony of psychological insights and forensic details. The impact of profiling on investigations can be likened to a detective gaining a sixth sense, offering a deeper understanding of the criminal mind.

One striking example is the hunt for the Unabomber, Ted Kaczynski. For years, his bombings eluded law enforcement. The breakthrough came with an FBI profiler's analysis, which painted a detailed picture of Kaczynski's personality and motivations. This profile was instrumental in focusing the investigation, leading to Kaczynski's eventual capture.

In the case of the Zodiac Killer, profiling played a significant, albeit more subtle, role. While the killer was never caught, the profiles created provided crucial insights into his behavior and motives, guiding detectives in their long and arduous investigation. The Zodiac case stands as a testament to how profiling can contribute to understanding the criminal psyche, even in the absence of an immediate arrest.

The role of profiling in solving the Anchorage Killer case is another exemplary instance. Israel Keyes, a meticulous and elusive predator, was ultimately apprehended due to a confluence of traditional detective work and profiling that narrowed down the type of individual capable of such crimes. The profile helped focus the investigation, leading to Keyes' eventual capture and confession.

These examples underscore the transformative effect of profiling in criminal investigations. It has provided law enforcement agencies with an invaluable tool in understanding the intricacies of the criminal mind, often pointing them in directions they might not have considered otherwise. The contribution of profiling to solving some of the most perplexing criminal cases in history is a vivid illustration of its impact and potential in the realm of criminal justice.

Clinical Analysis of Profiling Accuracy

The accuracy of criminal profiling in serial killer cases has been a subject of rigorous clinical analysis, examining the scientific underpinnings and effectiveness of this investigative tool. Clinical scrutiny of profiling techniques involves a methodical evaluation of their reliability and validity, often through retrospective analysis of solved cases.

One critical aspect under examination is the hit rate of profiles, which refers to the frequency with which predictions in a profile are accurate and helpful in leading to an arrest. Studies have shown varying results, with some indicating a relatively high hit rate, while others suggest more modest success. The variability in these findings points to the complexity of profiling and the multitude of factors that can influence its effectiveness, including the skill of the profiler, the nature of the crime, and the availability of detailed crime scene information.

Another area of clinical analysis focuses on the comparison between profiles and the actual characteristics of apprehended serial killers. These studies typically involve matching the profiles created before an arrest with the known traits of the convicted criminal. Findings often reveal a mix of accurate and inaccurate predictions, highlighting the challenge of creating a precise psychological and behavioral portrait of a largely unknown individual.

Clinical studies also investigate the utility of profiling in the investigative process. It is assessed not only in terms of leading directly to an arrest but also in its ability to narrow down suspects, provide new investigative leads, and prioritize resources effectively. This broader view of profiling's utility underscores its role as one component in a comprehensive investigative approach rather than a standalone solution.

The clinical analysis of profiling accuracy is an ongoing endeavor, with new methodologies and technologies continuously being integrated into the practice. These studies are crucial for understanding the strengths and limitations of profiling and for guiding its future development, ensuring that it remains a scientifically grounded tool in the arsenal against serial crime.

R: *Gary Ridgway*

The Green River Killer: Emergence

In the shadowy outskirts of Seattle, a predator lurked, his presence heralding a reign of terror that would stain the 1980s and '90s with blood and horror. Gary Ridgway, known infamously as the Green River Killer, wove a tapestry of death through the Pacific Northwest, his actions painting a gruesome picture of brutality. The unsuspecting victims, often sex workers or runaways, were lured by his seemingly innocuous demeanor, unaware of the fatal trap they were walking into.

His hunting grounds were the seedy streets and the murky banks of the Green River, where hope often came to die. Here, Ridgway would engage his victims, his approach predatory yet masked by an everyday facade. The initial interaction, seemingly benign, would swiftly spiral into a nightmare. The terror that unfolded was methodical and chilling; Ridgway's grip on their throats not just a means to kill, but a demonstration of his absolute control over life and death.

The aftermath of his killings was a macabre ritual. The bodies, lifeless and discarded, were often dumped in forested or overgrown areas. These became his morbid sanctuaries, where he would return to engage in acts with the deceased. This necrophilic behavior was not just a perversion but a calculated tactic to satiate his urges and avoid capture. The Green River, once a symbol of natural beauty, transformed into a sinister landmark synonymous with these atrocities.

Each murder was a grotesque masterpiece, crafted with a cold and calculating precision. The strangulation, his signature method, was both intimate and monstrous, a personal connection twisted into an act of ultimate domination. His victims, in their final moments, faced a terror unimaginable, their lives extinguished by a man who walked among them as an unassuming shadow.

The legacy of the Green River Killer is a chilling reminder of the darkness that can lurk within the human soul. Ridgway's actions were a brutal testament to the depths of human depravity, leaving a trail of sorrow and unanswered questions.

The horror he inflicted echoes through the annals of true crime, a stark portrayal of the monstrous capabilities of a serial killer hidden in plain sight.

Hunting Grounds: The Green River Cases

Amidst the backdrop of the serene Green River, a gruesome saga unfolded, its chapters written in blood and fear. The riverbanks, a picturesque setting by day, transformed into a macabre stage by night, where the killer's twisted fantasies turned into harrowing reality. The women, often lured under the guise of companionship or assistance, found themselves ensnared in a deadly trap, their vulnerability mercilessly exploited.

The predator's method was brutally efficient; his victims' last moments were a terrifying struggle for air, their pleas for mercy lost amidst the cold indifference of their assailant. The lifeless bodies, carelessly discarded near the river, became a horrifying testament to the killer's contempt for human life. These were not just crime scenes but a morbid canvas on which he expressed his darkest impulses.

As dawn broke, the river's tranquil waters bore silent witness to the night's horrors. The discovery of each victim sent shockwaves through the community, the reality of a lurking monster slowly dawning upon the unsuspecting populace. The Green River, once a symbol of natural tranquility, now echoed with the echoes of unspeakable acts, its waters a grim reminder of the lives brutally extinguished.

With each heinous act, the killer's confidence grew, his appetite for violence seemingly insatiable. The pattern of killings revealed a chilling precision, a methodical approach that spoke of a mind twisted by perverse desires. The authorities, grappling with the growing body count, found themselves in a relentless game of cat and mouse, the elusive predator always one step ahead.

The Green River cases stand as a dark chapter in the annals of true crime, a series of killings that not only terrorized a community but also challenged the very notions of humanity and morality. The river's once peaceful shores were forever marred by the actions of a single man, his deeds a stark reminder of the evil that can lurk beneath the surface of the ordinary.

Patterns of a Predator

In the dark underbelly of Washington's nightscape, a chilling pattern emerged, woven by a predator whose actions defied human comprehension. His targets, selected with a cold, predatory efficiency, were women marginalized by society - their vulnerability exploited, their trust betrayed. Each encounter began with a deceptive normalcy, a ruse that quickly spiraled into a nightmare of violence and fear.

The predator's method was a signature of his depravity. He strangled his victims, a personal and intimate form of violence that extinguished their lives and left their bodies as discarded husks. This act of strangulation was not merely a means to an end but an expression of his twisted need for control and dominance over the vulnerable.

In the aftermath of these heinous acts, the predator displayed a morbid ritualistic behavior. He would revisit the sites where he had dumped the bodies, engaging in acts of necrophilia. These post-mortem violations were not just further desecrations of his victims; they were a grotesque affirmation of his power over them, even in death.

The geographical dispersion of the bodies revealed a meticulous and methodical approach. The killer knew these areas well, choosing locations that were secluded yet accessible, places where he could indulge in his monstrous acts with little fear of discovery. This knowledge of the terrain indicated a predator deeply rooted in the very community he was terrorizing.

As the body count rose, a macabre pattern took shape, sketching the portrait of a serial killer whose actions were guided by a dark and twisted logic. The Green River Killer, as he would come to be known, had established a pattern of predation that instilled fear and horror in the heart of Washington state, a pattern that would challenge law enforcement and haunt the community for years to come.

Ridgway's Capture and Confessions

The end of the Green River Killer's reign of terror began not with a dramatic chase, but with the quiet advancement of forensic science. In the cold, analytical confines of a laboratory, DNA evidence silently tightened the noose around Ridgway. The breakthrough came when DNA from his saliva matched samples found on the victims, irrefutably linking him to the murders that had haunted Washington for decades.

Arrested on a bleak November day in 2001, the unassuming figure of Ridgway presented a stark contrast to the monstrous nature of his crimes. As he was led away in handcuffs, the communities he had terrorized for years breathed a collective sigh of relief, mixed with disbelief. The monster that had lurked in their midst was finally unmasked, his anonymity stripped away under the glaring light of justice.

In the interrogation room, Ridgway's confessions spilled out, a grotesque litany of murder and violation. He spoke with a chilling detachment, recounting his atrocities with the dispassion of a man disconnected from the very essence of humanity. Each confession peeled back layers of horror, revealing the depths of his depravity.

As part of a plea bargain to escape the death penalty, Ridgway led investigators to the hidden graves of his victims. These grim pilgrimages to secluded areas, where he had disposed of the bodies, were a stark testament to his methodical brutality. The recovery of these remains brought a somber closure to many families, even as it underscored the sheer scale of his murderous spree.

Ridgway's conviction and sentencing to life imprisonment without the possibility of parole closed a dark chapter in criminal history. His capture and confessions did not just signify the cessation of a killing spree; they marked the end of an era of terror and the beginning of a long, painful process of healing for the victims' families and the wider community.

The Psychology of Gary Ridgway

The twisted psyche of Gary Ridgway, the notorious Green River Killer, presents a chilling study in the depths of human depravity. His actions, driven by a complex web of psychological factors, painted a portrait of a man deeply entrenched in his own perverse world. Ridgway's early life was marred by a troubled family dynamic and personal issues, including a bedwetting problem and violent tendencies. These early experiences, coupled with a profound sense of inadequacy and anger towards women, set the stage for his later heinous acts.

His adult life was characterized by a deceptive veneer of normalcy, masking an undercurrent of dark desires. Ridgway's marriages, marked by infidelity and violence, were a reflection of his inner turmoil. His religious fervor, contrasting starkly with his predatory behavior, suggested a deep internal conflict. This juxtaposition of piety and perversion was a hallmark of his twisted personality, revealing a man struggling with conflicting impulses.

Ridgway's choice of victims and his method of killing highlighted his need for control and dominance. His targeting of vulnerable women and sex workers was not random but a deliberate choice, driven by a deep-seated misogyny and a desire to exert power over those he deemed inferior. The act of strangulation, a deeply personal and hands-on method, was a manifestation of his need to feel a physical and psychological dominance over his victims.

The psychological profiling by experts, including the work of FBI profiler John Douglas, offered insights into Ridgway's mind. The profile painted a picture of an individual with low self-esteem, a history of problems with women, and a familiarity with the areas where he dumped the bodies. This profiling played a crucial role in understanding the killer's mindset and ultimately led to his capture.

In summary, the exploration of Gary Ridgway's psychological landscape reveals a complex interplay of factors that culminated in his transformation into one of America's most notorious serial killers. His story is a grim reminder of the potential for darkness that resides within the human psyche, a darkness that, in Ridgway's case, led to unimaginable horror and suffering.

S: *Tommy Lynn Sells*

The Many Murders of Tommy Lynn Sells

Amid the chaos of his transient life, Tommy Lynn Sells transformed into a harbinger of death, his crimes painting a grisly tapestry across the American landscape. His modus operandi was as varied as it was vicious - a nightmarish blend of beating, raping, strangling, and stabbing. Each victim's tale was a unique atrocity, etched in blood and brutality. Sells, devoid of empathy, regarded humans merely as vessels of hatred. To him, they were nothing more than objects to satisfy his depraved urges, their lives extinguished with the same casual indifference with which one snuffs out a candle.

His first acknowledged murder, a horrific display of rage, occurred when he was a mere teenager. The act was perpetrated in Mississippi, where he claimed to have killed a man in a fit of fury. This unconfirmed kill marked the beginning of a two-decade-long spree, during which he crisscrossed the nation, leaving a trail of bodies in his wake. These early crimes were a prelude to the monstrous acts he would later commit, each more gruesome than the last.

One such chilling event unfolded in 1985, at a Missouri carnival. There, Sells encountered Ena Cordt and her young son Rory. After a night of intimacy, he woke to find Ena allegedly rummaging through his belongings. In a fit of rage, he grabbed the child's baseball bat and bludgeoned her to death, then mercilessly killed Rory to eliminate any witness to his atrocity. The bodies were discovered days later, by then Sells had vanished, a specter in the night.

October 1987 witnessed another of his ghastly deeds. Stefanie Kelly Stroh, a 21-year-old hitchhiker, became his prey as she journeyed through Nevada. Sells offered her a ride, a gesture of feigned kindness that soon turned deadly. In a secluded spot, he strangled her and disposed of her body in a hot spring, leaving no trace of her existence except for the haunting memory of her disappearance.

In November of the same year, the Dardeen family in Ina, Illinois, suffered a fate too cruel to imagine. Sells, having ingratiated himself with the family, unleashed an unspeakable horror within their home. He killed Russell Dardeen, then turned his sadistic attention to Russell's pregnant wife, Ruby Elaine, and their three-year-old son. The brutality of his attack caused Ruby Elaine to give birth during the assault, only for Sells to then murder the newborn. This heinous act, perhaps the most gruesome of his career, was a stark testament to the depth of his depravity.

Tommy Lynn Sells' story is not just a recounting of crimes; it's a descent into the darkest corners of human nature, a journey into the mind of a man who became the embodiment of pure evil. Each crime scene he left behind was a grotesque masterpiece of violence, a haunting reminder of the fragility of life and the presence of unfathomable darkness in the world.

Dissecting Sells: A Clinical Approach

Tommy Lynn Sells' psyche was a labyrinth of darkness, his mind a breeding ground for the most heinous of thoughts. Diagnosed with a complex array of mental disorders, he embodied the very essence of a disturbed individual. His actions were not mere criminal activities; they were the manifestations of a deeply troubled soul, tormented by an array of psychological ailments ranging from antisocial and borderline personality disorders to severe substance abuse and bipolar disorder. These diagnoses offer a glimpse into the chaos that reigned within him, driving him towards his dark deeds.

His childhood, marred by neglect, abuse, and trauma, laid the groundwork for his later atrocities. Early exposure to alcohol and narcotics warped his developing mind, setting him on a path of destruction. The lack of a stable, nurturing environment during these formative years was a crucial factor in shaping his twisted worldview. This turbulent upbringing was not just a backdrop to his crimes; it was the crucible in which his lethal tendencies were forged.

In his criminal career, Sells exhibited a disturbing detachment from his actions, an absence of remorse that is characteristic of severe antisocial behavior. He viewed his victims not as humans, but as objects to exert power over, reflecting a profound lack of empathy. This detachment was a hallmark of his psychological profile, revealing a deep-seated disdain for human life.

His confessions, a blend of truth and fabrication, were as much a part of his mental puzzle as the crimes themselves. Sells often claimed responsibility for murders he could not have committed, suggesting a craving for notoriety and recognition. This behavior raises questions about the veracity of his claims and points to a complex interplay of reality and fantasy in his mind.

In analyzing Sells, one delves into the mind of a man who was as much a victim of his mental afflictions as he was a perpetrator of unfathomable crimes. His life story serves as a stark reminder of the devastating impact of mental illness when left unchecked and untreated. Understanding his psychological makeup is not an exercise in absolution but an endeavor to comprehend the depths of human depravity.

A Mosaic of Murder: Sells' Widespread Victims

The trail of Tommy Lynn Sells was a macabre journey through America's heartland, marked by a mosaic of murder. Each crime scene was a tableau of terror, showcasing his ability to unleash violence with an almost artistic precision. His victims, diverse in age and background, were united in their tragic fates, becoming unwilling characters in his twisted narrative. From the innocence of a child to the vulnerability of a lone traveler, he preyed upon the unsuspecting, leaving behind a legacy of sorrow and unanswered questions.

The case of Ena Cordt and her son Rory, encountered at a Missouri carnival, epitomized his brutal opportunism. What began as a night of apparent trust ended in a bloodbath. The mother and child lay in their home, their lives extinguished by the merciless swings of a baseball bat - a weapon chosen for its cruel efficiency. This double homicide was not just a crime; it was a statement of his cold-bloodedness.

In Rockport, New York, the disappearance of Suzanne Korcz after leaving a bar alone morphed into a nightmarish reality when her remains were discovered near Niagara Falls years later. Sells' confession to this murder in 2004 painted a vivid picture of his ruthlessness and his perverse satisfaction in evading detection for so long.

The disappearance of Stefanie Kelly Stroh in Nevada offered a glimpse into his methodical approach to murder. Picking her up as a hitchhiker, he presented himself as a safe haven, only to extinguish her life and erase her existence in the depths of a hot spring. This act was not just a killing; it was an erasure of identity, a cruel theft of a future.

Sells' relentless spree of violence created a tapestry of terror across the nation, his crimes a series of dark, interconnected dots on the American landscape. His victims, each a story cut tragically short, left communities reeling and families forever broken. In understanding the breadth of his atrocities, one confronts the harsh reality of a predator moving undetected, his every step a potential prelude to horror.

The Invisible Killer: Evading Detection

Tommy Lynn Sells' ability to elude capture for decades was as chilling as the murders he committed. Moving ghost-like across the American landscape, he left a trail of devastation cloaked in anonymity. His transient lifestyle, hitchhiking and train-hopping, rendered him almost invisible to law enforcement, a specter slipping through the cracks of society. Each new town became a hunting ground, his presence there as fleeting as a shadow.

He mastered the art of blending in, working odd jobs that required no identification or lasting commitments. These roles were mere costumes, disguises he donned to hide his true nature. As a carnival worker or a barber, he observed his potential victims, learning their habits and vulnerabilities. His encounters were opportunistic, his exits strategic, ensuring no connection lingered long enough to draw suspicion.

In a sinister twist of fate, it was his attack on 10-year-old Krystal Surles in Texas that led to his downfall. She survived, a lone witness to his brutality, her testimony a beacon that guided investigators to his doorstep. This crucial slip shattered his shield of invisibility, pulling him into the glaring light of justice.

Yet, even in custody, Sells' enigmatic nature continued to confound. He wove tales of other murders, some verifiable, others likely fabrications. This game of truth and deception was his final act of defiance, a way to maintain control even as his freedom slipped away.

His arrest marked the end of a terrifying chapter in American criminal history. Sells' capture brought relief to a nation haunted by his crimes, but his shadow lingers, a dark reminder of the evil that can hide in plain sight.

The End of the Line: Capture and Conviction

The capture of Tommy Lynn Sells marked a critical juncture in his reign of terror. It was the sharp, sudden end to a long and bloody trail that had left communities across America reeling in fear. The pivotal moment came in Del Rio, Texas, when the youngest survivor of his brutality, 10-year-old Krystal Surles, bravely stepped forward. Her harrowing ordeal and miraculous escape provided law enforcement with the crucial lead they needed, leading them directly to the predator who had long lurked in the shadows.

His trial was a spectacle, a grim recounting of his myriad atrocities. The courtroom became a gallery of his gruesome deeds, with each testimony painting a vivid picture of his brutality. Families of the victims sat in stoic anguish, their faces etched with the pain of loss. The air was thick with sorrow and the overpowering desire for justice.

Sells, unrepentant to the end, offered no apology, no explanation for his actions. His stoic demeanor in the face of overwhelming evidence and anguished testimonies only served to amplify the horror of his crimes. He sat, an embodiment of unadulterated evil, a man who had relinquished his humanity long ago.

The sentence, when it came, was a foregone conclusion. The death penalty was more than a punishment; it was a societal imperative, a collective cry for closure from a nation shocked by the depth of his depravity. This sentence was not just the termination of a legal proceeding; it was the closing of a dark chapter in American criminal history.

With Sells' execution, a sense of finality descended. It was an end not just to his physical existence but to the lingering fear he had instilled. The death chamber at the Texas State Penitentiary in Huntsville became the final stage for the last act of his macabre life story. As the lethal dose was administered, a chapter of horror concluded, leaving behind a legacy of pain, loss, and the grim reminder of the human capacity for unspeakable evil.

T: *Ottis Toole*

Flames of Madness: Toole's Fiery Trail

Amid the stifling heat of a Florida summer, the air crackled with an ominous tension, foretelling the horror that was about to unfold. In a decrepit rooming house, the deranged mind of Ottis Toole found a perverse solace in the flickering flames he so adored. With a match's strike, he set the world ablaze, not just igniting the tinder-dry timbers but also the darkest corners of his twisted soul. The fire roared to life, consuming everything in its path, an insatiable beast that mirrored the arsonist's own insatiable appetite for destruction.

The inferno raged, a hellish symphony of crackling wood and shattering glass, as screams pierced the night. Toole watched, his eyes reflecting the fiery glow, a grotesque grin spreading across his face. Each scream, a macabre melody, seemed to fuel his sadistic desires further. The victims, trapped in the inferno's embrace, faced a terrifying ordeal, their fate sealed by the hands of a man whose heart was as cold as the ashes he would leave behind.

As the embers died, the gruesome aftermath revealed the true extent of the arsonist's depravity. Charred remains, barely recognizable as human, told a tale of unspeakable terror. The air, heavy with the stench of burnt flesh and despair, served as a haunting reminder of the atrocity committed. Toole, however, felt no remorse, his soul as barren as the scorched earth he left in his wake.

Yet, this was but one of the many scenes of carnage that the monster orchestrated. Each crime scene was a grotesque masterpiece, a testament to his twisted genius. The blood spattered walls, the dismembered bodies, the echoes of agony—all were brushstrokes in his macabre painting of pain and terror. With each victim, Toole delved deeper into his abyss of madness, his acts becoming more heinous, his methods more barbaric.

The partnership with Henry Lee Lucas only served to amplify his bloodlust. Together, they embarked on a depraved journey across the country, leaving a trail of blood and tears in their wake. Their crimes, a dance of death and destruction, were choreographed by the darkest impulses of the human psyche. Each murder, more vicious than the last, was a testament to their shared descent into the very depths of hell, a place from which there would be no redemption, only eternal damnation.

Confession and Controversy

In the dimly lit interrogation room, the air hung heavy with the scent of stale coffee and fear. Seated across from a seasoned detective, Toole's demeanor was unnerving in its calmness. His voice, when he spoke of his heinous acts, was devoid of emotion, as if reciting a grocery list rather than detailing the macabre tapestry of his life's work. Each confession peeled back the layers of a disturbed mind, revealing a soul so corrupted by evil that it defied understanding.

He reveled in the gory details, describing the way the knife felt in his hand, the sound of tearing flesh, and the sight of blood spilling onto the ground like some demonic offering. The detective, seasoned by years of exposure to the dark underbelly of humanity, found himself unsettled by the casual manner in which the killer recounted his atrocities. It was as if Toole was an artist, and murder was his craft, each victim a canvas upon which he expressed his twisted desires.

But as the hours wore on and the confessions piled up, a seed of doubt began to take root. The stories, though vivid and horrifying, were laced with inconsistencies and fantastical elements that strained credulity. The killer's eyes, once dull and lifeless, now sparkled with a perverse glee as he sensed the uncertainty in the room. Was he a master manipulator, weaving a web of lies to torment his captors, or was he truly the architect of the carnage he described?

The debate raged not only within the walls of that interrogation room but across the nation as the details of his confessions became public. Some saw him as a monster, a man whose capacity for evil knew no bounds. Others speculated that he was a pawn in a larger game, his confessions coerced or fabricated to close unsolved cases. The truth, elusive and shrouded in layers of deception and manipulation, seemed to slip further away with each passing moment.

In the end, the line between fact and fiction became irrevocably blurred. Toole's legacy was not just the blood he spilled but the questions he left in his wake. His life, a dark fable of violence and deceit, challenged our understanding of the human psyche and the depths to which it can sink. As the world looked on in horror and fascination, one thing became clear: the true story of Ottis Toole might never be fully known, a chilling reminder of the mysteries that lurk in the shadows of the human heart.

The Partnership in Crime: Toole and Lucas

The world seldom witnesses a duo as dark and destructive as Ottis Toole and Henry Lee Lucas. Their meeting was not just a fateful convergence of paths; it was the ignition of a human inferno. Together, they embarked on a blood-soaked journey, their crimes painting a tableau of terror across the American landscape. The bond they shared was forged in the depths of their mutual depravity, each egging the other on in a grotesque competition of cruelty.

In their twisted world, the pair found a disturbing kind of kinship. Toole, with his penchant for fire and mayhem, found a willing accomplice in Lucas, whose cold, calculating nature complemented his partner's chaotic impulses. Their crimes were not just acts of violence; they were perverse rituals. The victims, chosen at random, were mere props in their macabre play, each scene more horrifying than the last.

Lucas, the more manipulative of the two, often took the lead in their dance of death. He was the planner, the strategist, weaving their sinister web with a cunning that made their spree all the more terrifying. Toole, on the other hand, reveled in the carnage, finding a sick satisfaction in the visceral aspects of their crimes. His laughter, a chilling soundtrack to their brutality, echoed in the nightmares of those who investigated their heinous acts.

Together, they left a trail of bodies, each murder a testament to their shared insanity. The randomness of their attacks, the savagery of their methods, and the seeming lack of motive made them enigmas, shadows flickering on the periphery of understanding. Investigators scrambled to connect the dots, but with each discovery, the picture only grew more complex and disturbing.

Their eventual capture did little to dispel the darkness they had cast. In custody, the pair continued their twisted game, confessing to hundreds of murders, some of which were impossible for them to have committed. In the end, the true extent of their partnership in crime remained shrouded in mystery, a bloody legacy defined by the unspeakable horrors they perpetrated and the haunting questions they left unanswered.

U: *Unidentified Serial Killers*

The Long Island Serial Killer

The discovery at Gilgo Beach in 2010 unraveled a haunting saga of death, meticulously orchestrated by a predator lurking in the shadows of Long Island. Shrouded in secrecy, this killer's modus operandi revealed a chilling pattern – targeting sex workers, a vulnerable group often overlooked by society. The bodies, some decomposed to skeletal remains, were strategically placed, almost artistically, amidst the dense brambles and scrub of the beach's desolate landscape. Each victim, once a living, breathing person with hopes and dreams, was reduced to a cold statistic in the killer's grim collection.

As the sun dipped below the horizon on those fateful nights, a sinister figure emerged, driven by a grotesque compulsion. The killer's approach was both methodical and deeply personal; he knew the secluded spots, the perfect hunting grounds for his prey. The victims, lured by the promise of easy money, found themselves entrapped in a nightmarish reality. Their final moments were marked by terror, their cries muffled by the roaring Atlantic winds, as the killer exacted his twisted ritual.

In the killer's mind, the act of murder was an art form, each victim a canvas for his macabre masterpiece. The bodies were left posed, a grotesque display of his handiwork, hidden yet waiting to be discovered. The decomposition of the corpses, accelerated by the salty sea air, blurred the lines between human and nature, leaving a tableau morbidly intertwined with the landscape. This desecration of human life, a testament to the killer's deranged psyche, lay in stark contrast to the serene beauty of the beach.

The investigation into these heinous crimes hit numerous dead ends, the elusive killer always a step ahead. He seemed to vanish into thin air, his identity as enigmatic as the motives driving his bloodlust. The trail of clues - a shoe, a piece of jewelry, a tattered piece of clothing - were mere breadcrumbs leading investigators into an abyss of frustration and despair. Each discovery, a grim reminder of the lives brutally cut short, added layers to a puzzle far from completion.

With the arrest of Rex A. Heuermann, the veil of mystery began to lift, revealing the face of evil. The community, once plagued by fear and uncertainty, could now begin to seek closure. But the scars left by the Long Island Serial Killer run deep, the memories of the victims forever etched into the collective consciousness of a community forever changed by these horrific acts. The story of Gilgo Beach is not just a tale of murder; it's a somber reflection on the fragility of life and the darkness that can lurk within the human soul.

Jack the Ripper: A Mystery Unraveled?

The cobblestone streets of Whitechapel, soaked in the eerie fog of a London night, bore silent witness to the barbarity of Jack the Ripper. The air hung heavy with an unspeakable terror, palpable in every shadowy alley and dimly lit corner. The Ripper, an enigma shrouded in the dense mist, moved with a predator's grace, his intentions as dark as the night itself. Each victim, a tragic figure lost in life's hardships, met a gruesome end under the Ripper's merciless blade.

In those chilling autumn months of 1888, the Ripper's reign of terror left a bloody trail, each murder more horrifying than the last. The victims, their throats slit with surgical precision, bore the signature of a killer who reveled in the macabre. But it was the disembowelment, the cruel and unusual evisceration, that marked these murders as the work of a madman. The Ripper didn't just kill; he mutilated, his acts a gruesome tableau of human depravity.

The streets echoed with the whispers of the Ripper's deeds, each rumor more horrifying than the last. He was a ghost, a specter haunting the East End, his identity as elusive as smoke. The police, baffled and outmatched, grasped at shadows, their efforts hindered by the lack of forensic science. Witnesses spoke of a man, a mere wraith in the fog, but their descriptions varied, as if the Ripper was a chameleon, blending into the night.

The Ripper's letters, taunting the authorities with their cryptic messages, added a layer of twisted psychological warfare to his brutal physical acts. The ink, as red as the blood he shed, dripped with arrogance and contempt. He boasted of his deeds, his words a chilling insight into the mind of a monster. The letters were a game, a cat-and-mouse chase where the Ripper always seemed to be one step ahead.

To this day, the identity of Jack the Ripper remains one of history's greatest mysteries. The theories abound, each more compelling than the last, but the truth remains buried in the past. The Ripper's shadow looms large over the annals of crime, his legacy a testament to the darkness that can reside in the human heart. His was a story not just of murder, but of a city gripped by fear, a community forever changed by a killer lost to time.

The Phantom Killer of Texarkana

In the spring of 1946, the twin cities of Texarkana were gripped by a fear so palpable it seemed to seep from the very trees that lined its streets. A phantom lurked in the darkness, a specter of death haunting lovers' lanes, leaving behind a trail of blood and unanswered questions. This unseen terror, known only as the Phantom Killer, transformed the night into a time of dread, where shadows held unspeakable horrors.

The killer's first attack, a brutal introduction to his reign of terror, set the tone for the nightmare that would unfold. Young couples, seeking solitude under the moonlit sky, became unwitting participants in a deadly game. Their moments of intimacy violently shattered, replaced by a struggle for survival against a merciless assailant. The air, once filled with the whispers of sweet nothings, now echoed with the sounds of struggle and pain.

Each attack was a display of the killer's ruthless efficiency and his disturbing penchant for violence. His methods were brutally simple yet terrifyingly effective, leaving the victims with little chance of escape or defense. The gunshots, quick and precise, were the final punctuation to each horrific act. The killer's ability to evade capture only added to the growing legend of his ghost-like presence.

The fear that gripped Texarkana was not just of the physical violence but of the unknown. The Phantom Killer was a faceless terror, his identity as elusive as a wisp of smoke. Theories abounded, each more outlandish than the last, but the truth remained hidden behind a veil of mystery. The police, desperate for a lead, found themselves chasing shadows, their efforts hindered by the lack of concrete evidence.

Today, the story of the Phantom Killer remains a chilling reminder of the darkness that can lurk in the human soul. The unsolved nature of the crimes adds an eerie quality to the tale, a narrative incomplete but filled with dread. The Phantom

Killer's legacy is not just the lives he took or the fear he instilled; it is the enduring mystery, a puzzle that remains unsolved, a haunting question echoing through the annals of true crime.

The Enigma of the Zodiac Killer

The Zodiac Killer, an elusive shadow cast over the late 1960s in Northern California, wove a tapestry of terror and mystery that remains unsolved to this day. This enigmatic figure, cloaked in anonymity, orchestrated a series of murders with a chilling blend of precision and theatricality. His cryptic messages and ciphers sent to media outlets added a layer of perverse intellectualism to his brutal acts, taunting law enforcement and captivating public fear.

In the dead of night, the Zodiac's victims, unsuspecting and vulnerable, encountered a fate marked by horror and brutality. The killer's approach was both unpredictable and strategic, striking in secluded areas where the screams of his victims would be muffled by the vast, indifferent expanse of the night. The moonlit landscapes, once serene and tranquil, became stages for his macabre performances, each scene meticulously planned and executed with cold-blooded efficiency.

The Zodiac's signature, a simple yet haunting symbol, became an icon of fear. It adorned the letters he sent, each one a grim testament to his deeds and a puzzle for the authorities. His ciphers, complex and enigmatic, were a challenge to the public, a game of wits where the stakes were life and death. The letters revealed a killer who reveled in his notoriety, a man whose thirst for recognition was as insatiable as his lust for blood.

Each murder was a brushstroke in the Zodiac's grand design, a violent expression of his twisted psyche. The randomness of his victims, the variety of his methods, all pointed to a killer who sought not just to kill, but to instill fear and confusion. He was a master of manipulation, both of his victims and the media, a puppeteer pulling the strings of a horrified community.

The Zodiac Killer's reign of terror left an indelible mark on the American psyche, a legacy of fear and fascination that endures. His identity remains one of the greatest enigmas in the history of American crime, a puzzle that continues to intrigue and horrify. The Zodiac's shadow still looms large, a specter of evil that haunts the collective memory, a reminder of the darkness that can hide behind the mask of the ordinary.

Psychological Profiling of the Unknown

The dark corridors of the human mind can harbor unspeakable horrors, as evidenced by the chilling case studies of unidentified serial killers. These enigmas of the criminal world, shrouded in the anonymity of their unsolved crimes, present a daunting challenge to psychological profilers. Their unknown identities add layers of complexity, forcing profilers to delve deep into the abyss of human depravity and violence.

Profiling these shadowy figures requires a foray into the psyche of the unknown, piecing together a mosaic of potential motives and behaviors. Patterns emerge from the grisly tapestries of their crimes: signatures, methods, and choices of victims. Each element is a clue, a whisper from the dark side of the human psyche, guiding profilers in their quest to understand the understandable.

The lack of empathy, a hallmark of these killers, manifests in the brutality of their acts. Childhood trauma, a recurring theme, lurks in the background, hinting at a genesis of the killer's twisted worldview. The desire for control, a powerful motivator, is often evident in the meticulous planning and execution of their crimes. These insights, though speculative, form the crux of a profiler's hypothesis, a theoretical portrait of a killer unseen.

The fascination with death and violence, a grim thread weaving through the killer's life, points to a deep-seated psychopathology. Profilers must navigate this dark terrain, hypothesizing the mental and emotional processes driving these killers. Each crime scene is a chapter of a story written in blood; a narrative told through the macabre language of murder.

In the absence of concrete evidence, psychological profiling becomes an indispensable tool in the ongoing battle against these elusive predators. It is a dance with the shadows, a relentless pursuit of understanding amidst a sea of uncertainty. The profiler's task is not just to identify the killer but to explore the deepest, darkest recesses of human nature, where reason meets madness and morality loses its way.

V: *Dorángel Vargas*

From Outcast to Cannibal

The descent of Dorángel Vargas into the abyss of cannibalistic serial killing was marked by a gruesome transformation from a marginalized homeless man to a predator stalking the unsuspecting in the shadows of San Cristobal's parks. His victims, often vulnerable and unnoticed by society, met their fate at the hands of a man who saw them not as humans, but as a source of sustenance. His method was primitive yet brutally effective, ensnaring those who strayed too close with a metal tube or rocks, instruments of death wielded with a feral efficiency.

As night fell over the city, the parks, usually havens of tranquility, became his hunting grounds. He lurked in the darkness, waiting for the solitary figure of a drunkard or a beggar to cross his path. The attack, when it came, was swift and merciless. The sound of crushing bones and muffled cries dissolved into the nocturnal symphony of the park, leaving behind a chilling void.

In the aftermath, a macabre ritual unfolded under the cover of darkness. He dissected his prey with a chilling detachment, selecting the choicest parts for consumption. Muscles from thighs and calves were his preferred cuts, prepared with a rudimentary yet chilling culinary precision. The remains, a grotesque testament to his acts, were disposed of carelessly – heads buried, bones scattered, the evidence of his savagery hidden yet palpable.

His capture revealed the full extent of his monstrosity. The discovery of his lair was a descent into a nightmarish tableau – human remains crudely stored, a horrifying collection of trophies from his human hunts. The air was thick with the stench of death, and the ground littered with evidence of his unspeakable acts. It was a glimpse into the mind of a man who had long forsaken his humanity.

Vargas' confession, a chilling narrative of his deeds, was devoid of remorse or empathy. His words painted a vivid picture of a man consumed by his own twisted desires, a being who saw others not as fellow humans, but as mere objects for his consumption. His lack of regret, his detachment from the gravity of his actions, was perhaps the most horrifying revelation of all.

The Macabre Reality of the Hannibal of the Andes

In the heart of the Andean city, a gruesome reality lurked beneath the veneer of everyday life. The predator, Dorángel Vargas, roamed with a chilling purpose, his actions casting a shadow over the unsuspecting city. Each night, as darkness enveloped the streets, his twisted desires came to life in the form of a hunt—a relentless pursuit of human prey.

The park, a place of solace by day, transformed into his macabre domain by night. Here, Vargas stalked his victims with a predatory precision, his eyes scanning for the next unfortunate soul. The air was heavy with the scent of fear and anticipation as he closed in on his prey. His victims, lost in their own world, remained oblivious to the lurking danger until it was too late.

His method was as brutal as it was efficient. With a swift strike of a metal tube or the crushing force of a rock, he brought down his targets. The violence of the attack was stark, leaving the victims helpless in their final moments. Their pleas for mercy went unheard, muffled by the uncaring night.

Once subdued, the horror of Vargas' actions unfolded in the darkness. With a cold detachment, he dismembered his victims, his hands skilled in the grotesque art of butchery. The park, once a place of life, echoed with the unspeakable acts of a man who had surrendered to his darkest impulses.

The remnants of his brutality lay scattered, a chilling testament to the horrors that had transpired. The dawn brought no solace, only the grim reality of a city haunted by the presence of a monster in human form, a predator who walked amongst them, hidden in plain sight.

The Capture of Vargas

The end of Vargas' reign of terror began as an unsuspecting morning unfolded in San Cristobal. Law enforcement, following a trail of whispers and rumors, converged on an area that was about to reveal the darkest of secrets. Their discovery sent ripples of horror through the community, unearthing a reality far beyond the ordinary citizen's worst nightmares.

In the dense underbrush near Vargas' makeshift abode, the grim evidence of his atrocities lay scattered. The ground, a macabre mosaic of decomposing remains and discarded personal effects, told a story of unspeakable brutality. The search team, seasoned in the ways of crime and punishment, found themselves grappling with the sheer scale of the carnage.

His capture was as unassuming as it was significant. Found in a state of deranged tranquility, Vargas presented a stark contrast to the chaos he had wrought. His calm demeanor belied the frenzy of his crimes, and as he was led away, a chilling silence fell over the scene.

The interrogation room bore witness to the unraveling of a mind consumed by darkness. His confession, delivered with a disconcerting nonchalance, painted a vivid portrait of his gruesome escapades. Each word, devoid of remorse, added depth to the harrowing tale of a city's unseen nightmare.

As the news of his capture spread, a collective shudder ran through the city. The monster that had haunted their streets was no longer a shadow but a flesh-and-blood reality. His apprehension marked the end of a chapter of fear, but the scars he left behind would forever linger in the annals of San Cristobal's history.

Vargas' Confession and Trial

In the sterile confines of a courtroom, a hushed audience listened as Vargas, devoid of any visible remorse, recounted his heinous acts. His voice, eerily calm, detailed the macabre rituals he performed on his victims. The gallery, filled with a mix of curiosity and revulsion, hung on every word, as he described selecting and preparing human flesh with the same casual tone one might use to discuss a mundane task.

Prosecutors presented evidence that was as overwhelming as it was horrifying. The jury was subjected to graphic images and descriptions, each piece a fragment of the twisted puzzle that was Vargas' reign of terror. His lack of empathy, displayed in stark contrast to the tears and gasps from the gallery, underscored the depth of his depravity.

Defense arguments centered on Vargas' mental state, painting a picture of a man driven by forces beyond his control. Psychiatrists took the stand, their testimonies delving into the dark recesses of his psyche, attempting to find an explanation, a reason behind the unfathomable. Yet, the clinical analysis seemed almost inadequate in the face of such raw brutality.

The verdict, when it came, was a foregone conclusion. The weight of the evidence, the severity of the crimes, and the public outcry left little room for doubt. Vargas, the man who had instilled fear in the heart of a city, was found guilty on all counts.

As the sentence was pronounced, a sense of closure enveloped the courtroom. For the families of the victims and the city at large, it was the end of a nightmare. However, the shadow of Vargas' crimes would long linger, a dark reminder of the depths to which humanity can sink.

The Mind of Dorángel Vargas

Delving into the psyche of Dorángel Vargas, clinicians faced the daunting task of untangling a web of psychopathology steeped in violence and cannibalism. Their assessments revealed a man whose reality was a far cry from the norm, a mind that functioned on principles alien to the average person. The term 'paranoid psychopath' was frequently cited, an attempt to categorize a mind that defied conventional understanding.

Experts testified to his distorted perception of morality and humanity, a worldview where the lines between predator and prey were not just blurred but wholly nonexistent. They spoke of a man who, in his own twisted logic, saw his actions as a means of survival, a natural instinct rather than the abhorrent crimes they were. This chilling rationalization offered a glimpse into the depth of his detachment from societal norms.

His childhood, marked by isolation and possible exposure to guerilla warfare, emerged as a critical factor in his psychological development. Witnesses described a young Vargas as being different, his behavior increasingly erratic and violent as he grew. This background painted a picture of a life marred by trauma and instability, factors that likely contributed to his descent into criminality.

The clinical analysis, while comprehensive, struggled to fully encapsulate the enormity of Vargas' actions. Psychiatrists grappled with the challenge of explaining his cannibalistic tendencies, a rare and deeply disturbing aspect of his crimes. They delved into theories of mental illness, sociopathy, and the impact of extreme environmental conditions, yet the true essence of his motivations remained shrouded in mystery.

Ultimately, the study of Vargas' mind raised as many questions as it answered. It confronted the disturbing reality that within the human psyche lies the potential for unimaginable horror. His case stands as a stark reminder of the depths of depravity that can exist in a human being, a testament to the dark corners of the mind that most dare not explore.

W: *Women Who Kill*

Beyond the Stereotype: Understanding Female Serial Killers

Delving into the realm of female serial killers shatters the conventional image of a serial murderer. These women, often cloaked in an aura of normalcy, maternal warmth, or charismatic charm, defy the stereotype of a serial killer as a socially awkward, visibly disturbed male figure. Their methods and motives reveal a chilling calculation and manipulation of societal expectations.

Historically, female serial killers have been overshadowed by their male counterparts, not only in their infamy but also in the nature of their crimes. They tend to kill over a longer period, with less physical evidence and a more intimate connection to their victims. This extended duration of criminal activity often correlates with a deeper psychological entanglement in their crimes.

One of the most defining characteristics of female serial killers is their choice of victims and methods. They are more likely to target people within their care or close social circles, such as family members, lovers, or those they are entrusted to care for. Poisoning, a method that requires a certain level of intimacy and trust, emerges as a favored technique, offering a stark contrast to the more confrontational methods typically employed by male serial killers.

The underlying motives of female serial killers are as diverse as their methods. While some are driven by financial gain, others are propelled by a warped desire for control or a deep-seated psychological disturbance. Aileen Wuornos, for instance, claimed her murders were acts of self-defense against abusive clients, while Dorothea Puente ran a boarding house where she drugged and robbed her elderly tenants, reflecting a blend of financial motive and callous disregard for human life.

Understanding female serial killers requires a departure from the traditional narratives of serial murder. It calls for a nuanced exploration of the intersection between gender, psychology, and crime, unraveling the complex tapestry of factors that lead these women down a path of repeated, lethal violence. The examination of such cases not only broadens our comprehension of serial murder but also challenges the gendered perceptions of violence and criminality.

Infamous Cases: Women in the Annals of Serial Murder

The annals of crime brim with chilling tales of female serial killers, whose deeds have etched their names into the darkest corners of history. These women, weaving a tapestry of terror and deceit, have committed acts that defy the typical understanding of female behavior in society.

Belle Gunness, a Norwegian-American, presents a case steeped in mystery and horror. Operating at the turn of the 20th century in La Porte, Indiana, Gunness lured numerous suitors through personal ads only to brutally murder them for their assets. Her farmhouse, which later burned down under mysterious circumstances, revealed the grisly remains of several victims, casting a shadow of dread and disbelief across the nation.

In England, the shadow of Mary Ann Cotton looms large. Dubbed "The Black Widow," Cotton's reign of terror in the 19th century involved the calculated poisoning of up to 21 individuals, including her own children, husbands, and lovers. Her choice of arsenic, a subtle and easily disguised poison, allowed her to kill undetected for years, weaving a web of death under the guise of misfortune and illness.

Then there's Aileen Wuornos, an American prostitute turned serial killer in the late 20th century. Her life and crimes, marked by a tragic and abusive past, culminated in the murder of seven men. Wuornos' case became a media sensation, not only for the brutality of her crimes but also for the socio-psychological narrative that surrounded her life, challenging the norms of how society perceives female criminals.

The case of Juana Barraza in Mexico City brings a unique and horrifying twist to the narrative. Known as "La Mataviejitas" or "The Old Lady Killer," Barraza was a professional wrestler who targeted elderly women, robbing and murdering them in a series of attacks that shook the community and baffled investigators for years.

These women, though vastly different in their backgrounds, methods, and motives, are united by the sheer audacity and cold-bloodedness of their crimes. Their stories, woven into the fabric of criminal history, continue to fascinate and horrify, serving as stark reminders of the capacity for evil that resides in the human psyche, regardless of gender.

Motives and Methods: How Female Killers Differ

The study of female serial killers reveals a stark divergence in both the motives and methods when compared to their male counterparts. This divergence not only challenges the typical profiles of serial murderers but also provides a deeper understanding of the complex psychological and sociological factors at play.

Female serial killers often employ methods that are less confrontational and more surreptitious than those used by men. Poison, for instance, is a common tool in their arsenal. This method allows for a degree of detachment and manipulation, aligning with societal perceptions of women as nurturers or caregivers, roles that often afford them close and trusted contact with their victims. The use of poison also reflects a strategic approach, as it can be administered without immediate suspicion, allowing the killer to remain undetected for a longer period.

The motives driving female serial killers can be multifaceted, transcending simple categorizations. While financial gain is a significant factor, as seen in the cases of women who kill family members for insurance payouts or inheritance, there are also more complex psychological motivations at play. Some female serial killers are driven by a pathological need for control and dominance, often over those who are vulnerable or dependent on them. This need can stem from a history of abuse or trauma, leading to a twisted form of empowerment through the act of killing.

Another notable aspect is the relationship between the killer and her victims. Female serial killers often target those within their immediate social or familial circle. This pattern contrasts sharply with male serial killers, who frequently target strangers. The choice of victims close to the killer adds a layer of betrayal and deceit to the crimes, further complicating the psychological analysis.

Furthermore, the sexual element often present in male serial killings is typically less pronounced in female-perpetrated murders. When present, it is usually more about power and control than sexual gratification. This difference underscores the varied pathways and motivations that lead to serial murder, challenging the often oversimplified and gendered narratives surrounding these crimes.

In summary, the study of female serial killers requires an examination that goes beyond the mere comparison with male killers. It necessitates a thorough understanding of the unique social, psychological, and cultural factors that shape their crimes, painting a more complete and nuanced picture of serial murder as a whole.

Media Portrayals vs. Reality: The Female Killer in Popular Culture

The portrayal of female serial killers in media and popular culture often diverges dramatically from reality, creating a distorted lens through which these individuals are viewed. Films, television series, and books frequently depict these women as either monstrous anomalies or seductive temptresses, neglecting the complex and often mundane reality of their true nature.

In cinema and television, the female killer is often sensationalized, imbued with an almost mythic quality. They are portrayed as master manipulators, using their femininity as a weapon to ensnare unsuspecting victims. This portrayal taps into deep-seated societal fears and fascinations, creating a figure that is both feared and fetishized. The case of Aileen Wuornos, for instance, has been dramatized in films like "Monster," where her brutal murders are interwoven with a narrative of personal trauma and societal marginalization, offering a skewed yet captivating portrayal.

Literature, too, plays a significant role in shaping the perception of female serial killers. Here, they are often depicted as figures of horror or intrigue, their crimes serving as a backdrop for thrilling narratives. These depictions, while engaging, rarely delve into the psychological complexity or the banal reality of these killers' lives, instead focusing on the sensational aspects of their crimes.

This sensationalism stands in stark contrast to the actual profile of most female serial killers. In reality, these women are more likely to be unassuming figures, their outward normalcy allowing them to evade suspicion. Their methods, typically less gory and more covert than those of male killers, seldom make for the dramatic scenes favored in popular media.

The discrepancy between media portrayals and reality creates a gap in public understanding. While the dramatized versions of female killers capture public imagination, they often overshadow the more mundane, yet equally disturbing, truth. The sensationalism and glamorization can also lead to a trivialization of the victims' suffering and a skewed perception of the seriousness and complexity of these crimes.

Understanding the real dynamics of female serial killers requires peeling back the layers of media portrayal to reveal the less glamorous, but far more instructive, reality. It is in the unvarnished truth of their actions, motives, and personalities that one can begin to comprehend the profound implications of their crimes in society.

Analyzing the Psychology: Female Serial Killers in Focus

The psychological landscape of female serial killers is a complex terrain, marked by a convergence of various factors including personal history, psychological disorders, and societal influences. Analyzing these elements offers critical insights into the minds and motivations of these individuals.

One of the key aspects to consider is the role of trauma and abuse in the early life of many female serial killers. Studies have shown that a significant number of these women experienced severe physical, emotional, or sexual abuse during their formative years. This history of trauma can lead to a range of psychological disorders, such as borderline personality disorder, psychopathy, or post-traumatic stress disorder. These conditions can influence their perceptions and interactions with the world, often resulting in a distorted view of relationships and a skewed moral compass.

The psychological profile of female serial killers frequently reveals a deep-seated need for control and power. Unlike their male counterparts, whose killings are often driven by sexual gratification, women who commit serial murders are more likely to be motivated by a desire for dominance over their victims. This need for control can be a response to the helplessness and lack of control they experienced in their own lives, leading to a pathological inversion of their victimhood.

Another factor is the influence of societal and cultural norms. Women, traditionally viewed as nurturers and caregivers, can exploit these roles to facilitate their crimes. The societal reluctance to suspect women of such heinous acts can also play into their hands, allowing them to operate undetected for longer periods. This societal bias can be a double-edged sword, however, as it also leads to more sensationalized and stigmatized reactions when a woman is revealed to be a serial killer.

In addition to these factors, some female serial killers exhibit traits of mental illness, such as schizophrenia or bipolar disorder. These conditions can distort their reality and impede their ability to empathize with their victims, further facilitating their criminal behavior.

The study of female serial killers from a psychological perspective is not just about understanding their motivations or mental state; it is also about recognizing the broader implications for criminal profiling, law enforcement, and societal perceptions of women and violence. It challenges the traditional narratives of female passivity and male aggression, providing a more nuanced view of the capacities for violence across genders.

X: *The X-Factor in Serial Killing*

Defining the X-Factor: Unraveling the Unknowns

The concept of the "X-Factor" in serial killing represents an enigmatic blend of psychological, biological, and environmental factors that converge to create a serial killer. Unlike traditional criminal profiling, which often relies on known patterns and evidence, the X-Factor delves into the less tangible aspects of a killer's psyche and history. Renowned criminologists have long debated the weight of inherited traits versus acquired behaviors in the development of a serial killer. Studies suggest a complex interplay where genetic predispositions, when combined with specific environmental triggers, can lead to the emergence of a serial killing behavior. This intricate dance between nature and nurture forms the crux of understanding the X-Factor.

The Role of X-Chromosome Abnormalities in Criminal Behavior

In the labyrinth of genetic research, the role of X-chromosome abnormalities in shaping criminal behavior emerges as a topic of profound intrigue. Scientists have discovered that certain genetic mutations, particularly those affecting the X-chromosome, can influence aggressive and antisocial behaviors. For instance, the XYY syndrome, a rare chromosomal disorder, has been controversially linked with a predisposition to violent behavior. While not all individuals with this syndrome exhibit criminal tendencies, case studies like that of Richard Speck, who murdered eight nursing students in 1966, raise compelling questions about the genetic roots of brutality.

X Marks the Spot: Geographic Profiling in Serial Crimes

Geographic profiling stands as a pivotal tool in unraveling the mystery of serial crimes. This method involves analyzing the locations of a series of crimes to determine the most probable area of the offender's residence or operation base. The application of geographic profiling in cases like that of the Zodiac Killer, who terrorized Northern California in the late 1960s, illustrates its significance. By mapping the crime scenes, investigators can narrow down their search and understand the killer's spatial pattern, offering crucial insights into their behavior and movement.

The X-Files: Unresolved and Mysterious Cases

The realm of unresolved and mysterious cases, often referred to as the 'X-Files' of serial killing, holds a macabre fascination. These cases, shrouded in mystery, involve serial killers who have eluded capture, leaving a trail of unanswered questions and speculations. The case of Jack the Ripper, the infamous murderer of London's East End in the 1880s, remains one of the most enduring enigmas. The lack of concrete evidence and the myriad of theories that have emerged over the years underscore the complexity and elusive nature of such serial killers.

The Psychological X-Factor: Analyzing Unknown Motives

Delving into the psychological X-Factor of serial killers involves peeling back layers of their psyche to understand their unknown or unarticulated motives. Forensic psychologists often face the daunting task of reconstructing the mental landscape of these individuals. Factors such as childhood trauma, personality disorders, and neurological anomalies are scrutinized to piece together the puzzle. The case of Ted Bundy, known for his charm and intelligence, exemplifies the challenge of deciphering the psychological underpinnings of serial killers. Bundy's ability to mask his sadistic urges and blend into society poses critical questions about the nature of evil and the human mind.

Y: *Yang Xinhai China's Most Notorious Killer*

Brutality Unleashed: The Crimes of Yang Xinhai

Under the cloak of night, he prowled through the quiet, unsuspecting villages of rural China. His tools were simple yet horrifically effective: axes, hammers, and shovels. These instruments of terror were wielded with a brutal efficiency that chilled the soul. In each home he entered, a gruesome scene awaited the dawn. Families, once asleep in their beds, were found lifeless, their existences brutally extinguished. The killer moved like a shadow, his presence only felt in the cold aftermath of his violence.

In one harrowing incident, a father and his six-year-old daughter fell victim to his merciless onslaught. A shovel, an everyday tool, became an implement of unspeakable horror in his hands. In the same attack, a pregnant woman suffered grievously, her life forever scarred by his brutality. The juxtaposition of innocence and savagery in this act painted a portrait of a man lost to any semblance of humanity.

His attire for these nocturnal hunts was always methodically chosen: new clothes to avoid any trace, large shoes to mislead. The meticulous planning contrasted starkly with the chaotic violence of his crimes. This dichotomy revealed a mind that relished control yet reveled in disorder. Each crime scene was a tableau of this inner turmoil, a stark representation of a psyche untethered from moral constraints.

His capture, almost mundane in its execution, belied the enormity of his crimes. Detained during a routine police inspection, the horror of his actions unfurled in the interrogation room. The realization that he had been responsible for the longest and most gruesome killing spree in China's recent history sent shockwaves through the nation. The Monster Killer, as he came to be known, was a grim reminder of the depths to which humanity can sink.

Perhaps most chilling was his absence of motive, or rather, the futility of it. His reasons, initially speculated as revenge against society or the outcome of a broken relationship, eventually unraveled to reveal a more sinister truth. He killed because he wanted to, because it gave him a perverse sense of pleasure. His words, cold and devoid of remorse, echoed the darkness of his deeds: "When I killed people I had a desire. This inspired me to kill more. I don't care whether they deserve to live or not. It is none of my concern...I have no desire to be part of society. Society is not my concern." This chilling confession offered a glimpse into the abyss, a look at the void where a soul should have been.

Confessions of the Monster Killer

In the dimly lit confines of the interrogation room, the air hung heavy with the weight of impending revelations. He sat there, an enigma wrapped in human form, his eyes betraying nothing of the carnage he had wrought. As the questions began, his voice, eerily calm, started to unravel the tapestry of terror he had woven across the Chinese countryside. Each word, each confession, was a descent into the abyss of a murderer's mind.

He spoke of his first kill with a chilling detachment, as if recounting a mundane event. The night was quiet, the village unsuspecting, when he breached the sanctity of a humble abode. What transpired was a macabre dance of death, the farmer and his wife unsuspecting participants. Their final moments were a symphony of screams and the sickening thud of metal on flesh, a haunting melody that would echo across many more such nights.

As he recounted his crimes, a pattern emerged, one of meticulous planning and ruthless execution. He would scout out his next target, each a quiet village home, its occupants blissfully unaware of the nightmare about to unfold. With each retelling, the Monster Killer painted a portrait of a man who found solace in the screams of his victims, who sought out the rush of blood and the finality of death.

The depths of his depravity knew no bounds. In one particularly harrowing account, he described how he lingered in a family home after snuffing out all life within. Amidst the stillness of the aftermath, he sat and ate a meal, surrounded by the lifeless bodies of his victims. This grotesque act of post-murder normalcy unveiled a chilling facet of his psyche, a disconnect from humanity so profound it defied understanding.

His confessions laid bare not just the extent of his crimes, but also the darkness of the human soul. He expressed no remorse, no hint of regret. Instead, there was a sense of pride, a perverse satisfaction in his ability to instill fear and inflict pain. His final words in the interrogation room resonated with a bone-chilling clarity: "I am not of your world. I exist beyond the realm of your understanding." In those words lay the terrifying truth of a man who had become the very embodiment of a nightmare.

The Manhunt for a Monster

The hunt for the elusive killer stretched across the vast expanse of China, a nation grappling with the reality of a predator moving unchecked through its heartland. Law enforcement agencies, previously confounded by the seemingly random nature of the murders, began to piece together the grisly puzzle. Each crime scene offered new clues, painting a picture of a man who struck with ruthless precision, leaving communities in a state of paralyzing fear.

In the wake of his terror, a specialized task force was assembled, a blend of seasoned detectives and forensic experts. Their mission was singular: to track down the phantom who slipped through the night, leaving a trail of blood and sorrow. The task force delved into the psyche of the killer, analyzing his patterns, his choice of victims, and the brutal signature left at each crime scene. This deep dive into darkness was not just a hunt for a man; it was a race to stop a force of pure malevolence.

As the investigation intensified, the killer seemed to vanish, a ghost in the vast rural landscape of China. Tips and sightings poured in, each a potential lead that quickly turned cold. The frustration within the task force grew palpable, the weight of each unsolved murder a constant reminder of the urgency of their quest. The nation held its breath, each news report a beacon of hope in the grim saga.

The breakthrough came unexpectedly, a stroke of fate that tilted the scales. The killer, emboldened by his evasion of capture, made a critical error. A routine police inspection at an entertainment venue in Cangzhou, Hebei, unveiled the man behind the monster. His capture, far from the dramatic showdown many had envisioned, was anticlimactic, yet it marked the end of a reign of terror that had held a nation hostage.

With the killer in custody, the task force's work shifted from pursuit to preparation for trial. The evidence, meticulously gathered and preserved, formed a damning portfolio of his crimes. It was a testament to the determination and skill of the law enforcement teams, a small measure of solace for the families of the victims. The manhunt had ended, but the journey to justice was just beginning.

Yang Xinhai: A Clinical Examination

The dissection of Yang Xinhai's psyche offers a disturbing glimpse into the mind of a serial killer. Clinical psychologists tasked with understanding his motivations faced a daunting challenge. The layers of his personality, when peeled back, revealed a complex interplay of psychological disturbances. His acts were not mere outbursts of violence but were underpinned by a deep-seated malice and a detachment from societal norms.

His childhood, marked by poverty and a lack of familial warmth, emerged as a focal point in understanding his later descent into violence. Psychologists pointed to these formative years as a breeding ground for his emotional and social detachment. However, caution was exercised in drawing direct lines from his upbringing to his crimes, acknowledging that many endure similar hardships without resorting to violence.

The escalation of his criminal behavior, from theft to rape, and ultimately to serial murder, was indicative of a growing devaluation of human life. The clinical team delved into this progression, exploring how each act of violence further desensitized him. He exhibited classic signs of a psychopath: lack of empathy, remorselessness, and a failure to conform to social norms, all contributing to his heinous acts.

His interactions during imprisonment and trial were particularly telling. He showed no signs of remorse or understanding of the gravity of his actions. His responses were often cold, calculated, and devoid of emotional depth. This emotional void was a critical component of his psychological makeup, allowing him to commit acts of extreme brutality without the hindrance of conscience.

The final analysis painted a picture of a man deeply fractured by his own inner demons. While his crimes were his own, the examination offered insights into the broader conversation about the origins of such extreme criminal behavior. Understanding the mind of Yang Xinhai was not about finding excuses for his actions but about gaining knowledge to prevent future tragedies.

China's Most Notorious Killer

The tale of Yang Xinhai's reign of terror is etched deeply into the annals of criminal history. In the dead of night, he would emerge from the shadows, a harbinger of death and destruction. Homes that once resonated with the warmth of family life were transformed into scenes of unimaginable horror. His method of entry was silent, his attacks sudden and devastating. The villages of rural China, once havens of tranquility, became stages for his gruesome performances.

His victims, chosen at random, were ordinary people: farmers, rural families, those least expecting the nightmare that would unfold. He wielded his tools - axes, shovels, hammers - with a brutal precision, leaving behind a macabre tableau of splintered bones and spilled blood. The brutality of his crimes was not just in their execution but in the mercilessness with which he extinguished entire families, snuffing out generations in a single, bloody act.

The stark contrast between his quiet, laborer's exterior and the savage killer within confounded all who sought to understand him. He moved through the provinces of Anhui, Hebei, Henan, and Shandong, a specter of death, his true nature hidden beneath a facade of normalcy. Each murder was a meticulous act of violence, planned with a cold, calculating mind and executed with a savage glee.

His capture brought an end to the bloodshed, but it also opened a Pandora's box of questions. How could one man wreak such havoc? What drove him to commit acts of such unspeakable violence? The interrogation room's stark, fluorescent lights did little to illuminate the darkness that lay within his psyche. His confessions, delivered in a chillingly calm manner, offered a glimpse into the mind of a man who had strayed far from any semblance of morality.

Yang Xinhai, dubbed the 'Monster Killer,' left a scar on the collective consciousness of a nation. His crimes, a series of nightmarish vignettes, painted a portrait of a man who found solace in the suffering of others. In the annals of serial killers, he stands as a stark reminder of the depths of depravity to which a human being can descend, a symbol of the unfathomable darkness that can lurk within the human soul.

Z: *Zhang Yongming*

The Carnage Unveiled

Amidst the shadows of predation, a chilling tableau unfolds, a gruesome mosaic of death and depravity. The serial killer, a harbinger of doom, enacts his macabre dance upon the unsuspecting. Each victim, a silenced testimony to his unyielding cruelty. Streets once bustling with life now whisper tales of terror, as bloodstains and unanswered cries linger in the air. Here, the predator's true nature is revealed: not just a murderer, but an artist of death, crafting each scene with meticulous, horrifying detail.

In this grotesque gallery, the killer's methods vary, each crime scene a unique, horrifying masterpiece. With cold, calculating precision, he manipulates flesh and bone, leaving behind a trail of mutilated bodies. Organs are displaced with chilling intent, limbs arranged in grotesque parodies of their former grace. The air, heavy with the scent of iron and fear, tells a story of pain and final moments spent in unspeakable agony.

In one macabre scenario, the killer transforms an ordinary room into a canvas of carnage. Blood spatters paint the walls in a symphony of scarlet, each droplet a note in a song of suffering. The body, central to this horrific scene, is splayed with deliberate care, exposing the inner workings of a once-living being. Here, the boundary between life and death blurs, and the killer's perverse fascination with the human form is laid bare.

Nightfall brings no respite, as the darkness becomes his ally. Under the cloak of night, he hunts, his footsteps silent, his intentions deadly. Each victim, chosen with a predator's instinct, becomes part of a nightmarish ritual. The moon, a silent witness to these unspeakable acts, casts a pale light on scenes of chaos and despair. In these moments, the killer is both specter and executioner, a ghostly presence leaving behind a legacy of horror.

As dawn breaks, the aftermath of his savagery is revealed in the harsh light of day. The community, paralyzed by fear, struggles to comprehend the extent of the brutality. Families mourn, their lives forever altered by loss, while law enforcement grapples with the enormity of the crimes. The killer, meanwhile, recedes into the shadows, his identity shrouded in mystery, his thirst for blood unquenched. In this relentless cycle of violence, each act more vicious than the last, the killer's dark journey continues, his story written in the blood of his victims.

Echoes of Horror

In the dead of night, the streets become a hunting ground. Shadows merge with the darkness as the killer moves with predatory grace, his eyes scanning for the next victim. The city, alive with the hum of unsuspecting lives, remains oblivious to the lurking menace. His approach is silent, his movements calculated – each step a closer descent into the abyss of his twisted desires.

The moment of attack is both sudden and brutal. Victims, caught in the grips of an ordinary evening, find themselves thrust into a nightmare. Their screams, muffled and short-lived, are the only testament to their final struggle. The killer's hands, instruments of death, are unyielding and precise. Blood, warm and vibrant, stains his fingers, a visceral reminder of the life he extinguishes.

In the aftermath, the crime scenes speak volumes of the killer's mind. Each location is carefully chosen, a stage set for the macabre performance. Bodies are displayed with grotesque attention to detail, wounds gaping like silent screams. The air is thick with the metallic tang of blood, mingling with the stench of decay. These scenes are not mere displays of violence, but a twisted form of communication from the killer to the world.

As dawn breaks, the gruesome discoveries send shockwaves through the community. The brutality of the acts is incomprehensible, leaving a trail of questions and fear. Families are shattered, their grief a palpable entity in the wake of such savagery. The law enforcement, faced with the daunting task of piecing together the horror, delve into the mind of a monster, hoping to predict his next move.

Yet, with each passing day, the killer remains a step ahead, his identity shrouded in secrecy. The city, once a bustling hub of life, now whispers tales of the unseen terror. Eyes are watchful, hearts are heavy, as the realization sets in: the killer walks among them, his thirst for violence unquenched, waiting for the cover of night to claim his next victim.

Shadows of a Predator

In the heart of the city, under the guise of darkness, a predator roams. His footsteps are silent, blending with the night as he stalks his prey with chilling precision. The streets, alive with the innocent and the oblivious, provide a canvas for his dark desires. Each potential victim is observed, evaluated, a pawn in his deadly game of cat and mouse.

The moment of attack is a crescendo of horror. Victims, engrossed in their mundane routines, are suddenly plunged into a world of terror and pain. Their struggles, futile against his overpowering force, end quickly, leaving behind a haunting silence. His methods are methodical, each movement deliberate, ensuring his gruesome message is clearly articulated.

Post-mortem, the scenes he leaves are meticulously arranged tableaus of terror. Bodies are positioned in grotesque displays, a macabre signature of his handiwork. Blood, once pumping life, now pools around his artistry, a stark contrast to the stillness of death. These crime scenes are not just evidence of murder but a glimpse into the mind of a man who finds beauty in brutality.

As the sun rises, revealing his night's work, a wave of fear washes over the community. The sheer savagery of the scenes leaves a scar on the collective psyche. Families mourn, their sorrow a deep chasm of loss and despair. Detectives, tasked with making sense of the senseless, delve into the abyss, trying to trace the steps of a killer who seems to vanish with the light.

Yet, the city remains unaware of the monster in their midst. With each setting sun, a renewed sense of dread descends. People lock their doors, glance over their shoulders, the terror of the unknown looming large. He watches, waits, his hunger for the hunt undiminished. In this deadly game of shadows, he is always one step ahead, his next move a mystery, his identity a question mark written in the blood of his victims.

The Hunter's Moon

Under the hunter's moon, the city's façade of safety shatters. Here, the killer moves like a ghost, his presence only felt in the wake of his atrocities. The night air, usually filled with the sounds of life, now carries an ominous stillness. His victims are not chosen at random; each one is selected with a predator's instinct, a piece in his twisted game.

His attacks are a brutal symphony of violence. Victims, once symbols of vibrancy and life, are reduced to mere objects in his ritual of death. Their final moments are a blur of fear and confusion, a dance with death that ends in a silent scream. He is meticulous, leaving no trace of his identity, only the evidence of his dark desires written in blood and gore.

At each crime scene, the killer's signature is unmistakable. Bodies are displayed in ghastly arrangements, their wounds a testament to his savagery. The scenes are more than just killings; they are messages from the killer, a demonstration of his power over life and death. The air is thick with the scent of blood, a metallic reminder of the horror that transpired.

With the break of dawn, the city awakens to a new nightmare. The community reels in shock, the reality of the killer's actions a gaping wound in the fabric of society. Families are left in ruins, their grief a heavy shroud of despair. Detectives are pulled into the killer's twisted world, each clue a piece of a puzzle that seems impossible to solve.

As night falls again, a sense of dread settles over the city. The killer, his identity hidden in the shadows, watches and waits. He is the master of this nocturnal realm, his hunger for the hunt undiminished by his previous conquests. With each victim, he writes a new chapter in his book of horrors, the city his unwilling co-author in a story of unspeakable terror.

Veil of Darkness

As night descends, a veil of darkness cloaks the city, turning familiar streets into a stage for horror. In this obscurity, the serial killer finds his element, a shadow among shadows, his steps soundless as he prowls. The city, alive with unsuspecting souls, is oblivious to the monster in their midst, each individual a potential chapter in his grisly narrative.

With each attack, the killer crafts a scene of visceral terror. His victims, plucked from the mundane safety of their lives, are thrust into a maelstrom of pain and fear. Their struggles, desperate and futile, end in a crescendo of silence. In these moments, he is both artist and executioner, his methods a ghastly display of control and precision, leaving behind a tableau steeped in blood and horror.

The aftermath of his deeds paints a picture of stark brutality. Crime scenes are meticulously arranged, a grotesque testament to his handiwork. Bodies, mutilated and defiled, are positioned with a sickening attention to detail, transforming them into macabre sculptures. These sites are not mere locations of death; they are the killer's canvas, each telling a story of brutality and madness.

With the break of dawn, the city awakens to the aftermath of his nocturnal pursuits. The community, once a tapestry of vibrant life, is now marred by the specter of his actions. Families are plunged into an abyss of grief, their loss an unending echo of sorrow. Law enforcement, faced with deciphering his macabre clues, ventures into the depths of his twisted psyche, seeking to anticipate his next move.

Yet, as the sun sets, the cycle begins anew. The killer, a phantom in the twilight, watches with cold anticipation. His hunger for the hunt remains insatiable, each act of violence a continuation of his grim saga. In this game of cat and mouse, he is always a step ahead, his identity a puzzle cloaked in bloodshed, his story a nightmare written in the lives of his victims.

Made in United States
Orlando, FL
05 March 2024

44429693R00134